GENDER, PENSIONS AND THE LIFECOURSE

How pensions need to adapt to changing family forms

Jay Ginn

The POLICY PRESS

First published in Great Britain in June 2003 by

The Policy Press
University of Bristol
Fourth Floor, Beacon House
Queen's Road
Bristol BS8 1QU
UK

Tel +44 (0)117 331 4054
Fax +44 (0)117 331 4093
e-mail tpp-info@bristol.ac.uk
www.policypress.org.uk

British Library Cataloguing in Publication Data

A catalogue record for this book is available from the British Library

ISBN 1 86134 338 8 hardback

A paperback version of this book is also available

Jay Ginn is Senior Research Fellow and Co-Director of the Centre for Research on Ageing and Gender, Sociology Department, University of Surrey.

Cover design by Qube Design Associates, Bristol.
Front cover: photographs supplied by kind permission of www.johnbirdsall.co.uk
Printed and bound in Great Britain by Hobbs the Printers Ltd, Southampton.

Contents

List of tables and figures

Tables

Figures

Acknowledgements

The impetus for writing this book was the neglect of gender issues in pensions policy debates, especially the pension disadvantage experienced by most British women due to their unpaid caring work over the lifecourse. The research on which this book draws was carried out during two projects in the Sociology Department of the University of Surrey, funded by the Leverhulme Trust (Ref F/242/4) and the Economic and Social Research Council (Award No R000271002). I am grateful to the Office for National Statistics for permission to use the General Household Survey data, to the Department for Social Security for permission to use the Family Resources Survey data and to the Data Archive, University of Essex, and to Manchester Computing Centre for access to the data. I am, however, responsible for the data analysis.

I am grateful to the Netherlands Institute for Advanced Studies for a Residential Fellowship to examine financial strategies of individuals in midlife. The Fellowship enabled me to complete the book, which also benefited from stimulating discussions at the Institute.

Thanks are due to colleagues at the Sociology Department, University of Surrey, for their help in reading and commenting on earlier versions of the chapters. First, Professor Sara Arber provided encouragement, advice and support during the research phase and also made many constructive suggestions concerning the typescript. Chapter Four benefited from Debora Price's comprehensive knowledge of the British pension system, especially in legal and technical aspects, as well as her understanding of legislation surrounding divorce. Debra Street of the Pepper Institute for Aging at Florida State University gave generously of her precious time in reading all the chapters, asking pertinent questions and providing many helpful comments. Sue Ward of the Independent Pensions Research Group kindly helped with my queries on obscure aspects of occupational pensions. Any mistakes, of course, remain my responsibility.

Last but not least, I thank my friend and partner Chris for the dollops of humour that kept me going throughout the research and the writing.

ONE

Trends in gender relations, employment and pensions

As the main source of income in later life, pensions can make the difference between a daily struggle and a period of fulfilment, between merely surviving and actively thriving. At the start of the twenty-first century, life in retirement has lengthened, with people living an average of over 20 years beyond the state pension age. With longer lives, an adequate pension income is more necessary than ever before. Women's savings have to last longer than men's, as they can currently expect to live another 22 years after age 60 compared with 18 for men (OECD, 2001a).

There is a widespread sense of crisis and uncertainty over the future of pensions in Britain. While state pensions are apparently in terminal decline due to the policy of successive governments, the risks of reliance on the private sector of pensions are increasingly evident. Plummeting projections for investment returns and a question mark over the continuation of final salary occupational pension schemes follow a saga of mis-selling in personal pensions. Expressing widespread concern, one financial expert concludes that "The much-trumpeted UK model of private pensions funding looks distressingly shaky" (Plender, 2003, p 1). As a result, many people banking on their private pensions are threatened with an impoverished old age, or a much lower income than they expected. Both the government and the private pensions industry urge people to save even more in private pension schemes, to make up the shortfall. However, the ability to do this is gendered, depending on employment and earnings, and also varies with stage in the lifecourse.

Far-reaching social changes have transformed gender relationships and norms as to partnering and parenting. Major changes include growing expectations of women's equality and financial independence irrespective of marital status; the sexual revolution, giving women greater control over their fertility; and increasing recognition of the importance of women's skills in the workplace and the economy as a whole. At the same time, the expectation of lifelong marriage has declined, with increases in divorce, cohabitation and lone parenthood as all these have become more socially acceptable. These changes offer both opportunities and challenges to individuals and society and have profound implications for women's acquisition of pensions. Yet successive generations encounter (and contribute to) these changes at different stages in their lifecourse, with consequently different effects on their future options. For example, cohorts of women reaching adulthood in the 1960s were able to make choices concerning family planning and employment rarely available to those reaching adulthood in the 1940s. A later generation, entering the workforce in the 1980s, benefited from the equality legislation of the 1970s and from the ideas of second wave feminism that permeated society.

In the same way, as the British pension system evolves, each generation accumulates pension entitlements under new conditions, applying at particular stages of their life. Whereas the current older generation, and many now in midlife, expected state pensions to form a solid bedrock of retirement income (supplemented if possible by savings and private pensions), that bedrock is crumbling to sand for their successors. Just when increasing numbers of women are becoming entitled to the basic state pension in their own right, its value is falling further below the poverty line – the level of eligibility for means-tested income support. Increasingly, a substantial amount of private pension income (from occupational or personal pensions) will be required to avoid poverty in retirement. Such developments in the structure of the pension system, discussed more fully later in this chapter, may reinforce gender inequalities in prospects for a financially secure retirement, despite women's increasing participation in the labour market. The implications of pension policy are also important for men. Pension penalties – which are being deepened by the most recent developments – are imposed on all those, men or women, whose employment patterns are shaped by caring responsibilities.

Because of the long time frame involved in the accumulation of pension entitlements, the retirement income of each generation of women reflects both past reforms in pension arrangements and the changing norms about marriage, motherhood and employment prevailing during that generation's working life. Feminist analysis has barely begun to explore how changing gender roles interact with shifts in pension policy to structure income inequality in later life between men and women and also among women.

A political economy approach is used in this book. Thus a key concern is to analyse how British welfare policies alter the distribution of power, income and life chances, creating winners and losers in later life. Specifically, how does pension policy operate to construct life chances differently for men and women, and for different social groups within each gender? Changes over time in gender relations and in the pension system highlight new issues of distributional equity – between men and women, parents and the childless, partnered and lone parents, those who provide informal care and those who do not. The book sets out to explore these issues, using recent research on how employment and private pension acquisition vary according to gender, educational level, class, ethnicity, marital status, parenthood and birth cohort. A major focus is how changes and continuities in the gender division of labour and in patterns of partnering and parenthood shape gender inequalities in pension prospects.

In this chapter, the evolution of gender roles, trends in employment and earnings and the gender implications for pension acquisition are considered. Gender-relevant changes in the British pension system since 1940 are outlined, including recent reforms shifting the balance of pension provision towards the private sector. Debate as to the optimum balance of state and private pensions has taken on a new urgency as the inherent risk of pensions based on investment in the stock market becomes increasingly apparent.

Gender relations and older women's income

The disproportionate share of poverty borne by today's older women reflects the model of gender relations prevailing during much of their earlier lives, one in which a distinct gender division of labour confined most married women to raising a family and homemaking – the male breadwinner–housewife model. Married women of this generation, even those with some hours of paid work, expected to undertake the major share of domestic tasks, including the nurturing and socialisation of children and the care of other family members, freeing men to maximise their earnings and support their family. Before the 1950s, women were expected (or even required) to resign from their jobs on marriage, although later in their lifecourse employment became common. The result can be seen in the work histories of older women. Those who had ever been married had fewer years of employment and substantial periods of part-time, rather than full-time, work relative to never-married women and to men, with consequently low private pension income (Ginn and Arber, 1996). Longitudinal research has confirmed the profound effect of work history in differentiating later life incomes (Bardasi and Jenkins, 2002).

Figure 1.1: Individual income[a] of men and women aged 65+ by marital status

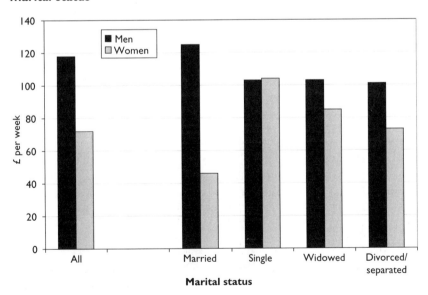

Note:[a] median gross income.

Source: Ginn and Price (2002) using data from the GHS 1994-96

As a result, gender differences in older people's income are substantial and three quarters of pensioners claiming means-tested financial support are women. Figure 1.1 shows median individual incomes of men and women over age 65 in the mid-1990s, distinguishing according to marital status. The median, which is the 'middle' value, is a better measure of the average than the arithmetic mean, because it is less influenced by extreme values. Older women's personal income was only about 60% of men's, on average. For example, in the mid-1990s, older women's median income was £72 per week, compared with £118 for men. Because older women are more likely than older men to live alone, with all the dis-economies entailed in solo living, these figures underestimate the gender difference in living standards. Older women's personal income varies with marital status, reflecting the way earlier family caring roles reduced their opportunity to contribute and benefit from pension schemes.

Figure 1.2: Private pensions of men and women aged 65+ by marital status

a) Percentage receiving a private pension

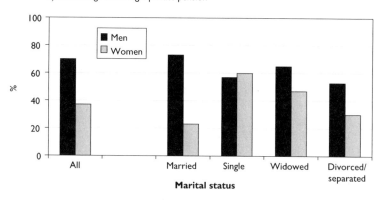

b) Median amounts for those with a private pension

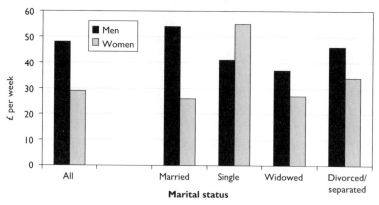

Source: Ginn and Price (2002) using data from the GHS 1994-96

This pattern of income inequality with gender and marital status arises mainly from differential receipt of private (occupational or personal) pensions. Only a third of older women have any private pension income, including widows' pensions based on their deceased husbands' private pensions, and the amounts are less than for men (see Figure 1.2). Among women with some private pension income, the amounts received by married, widowed and divorced women are low compared with single (never married) women. For the remaining two thirds of women, their entire pension income is through the state. In the 1990s, private pensions contributed 25% of older men's personal income but only 11% of women's (Ginn and Arber, 1999).

Will the apparent revolution in British women's employment over the past few decades enable working-age women to avoid the pension poverty their mothers and grandmothers are experiencing? What are the prospects for reducing gender inequality in later life income in the future? The next sections of this chapter consider how gender relations in Britain have evolved, and review current gender inequalities in employment and earnings over time.

Evolving gender relations

Despite changing attitudes towards gender roles and women's increased employment participation, in Britain the bulk of unpaid domestic and caring work is still performed by women (Gershuny et al, 1994; Murgatroyd and Neuburger, 1997; ONS, 2002a), constraining their employment opportunities while boosting those of married men (Gershuny, 1997). Most employed women work a 'second shift' of domestic labour (Hochschild, 1989), bearing the bulk of responsibility for childcare at the expense of their current and future earnings.

The reasons for the continuity in the gender division of domestic labour, and whether more radical change can be expected in the future, are matters of debate (Crompton and Harris, 1999). While Hochschild (1989) refers to a 'stalled revolution', noting that changes in the domestic division of labour do not match the increase in women's employment, Gershuny et al (1994) suggest 'lagged adaptation', in which men are merely slow to adjust to new realities by renegotiating domestic responsibilities. Other writers suggest the lack of change in women's share of domestic work is due to the persistence of male material dominance, combined with gender socialisation. An alternative perspective is offered by Hakim (2000) who argues that women's preferences – for building a home rather than a career – are the main reason for their disadvantages in the labour market. However, the majority of women try to maintain both employment and family, their employment behaviour reflecting external constraints as much as prior preferences (McRae, forthcoming).

It is not only men's failure to undertake an equal share of domestic work that influences women's opportunities in the labour market. The state's provision (or lack) of welfare services to complement and support family caring is also important in enabling women to engage in full-time employment (O'Connor et al, 1999). In liberal welfare states such as Britain and the US, policy has been contradictory, simultaneously urging women into paid employment while providing minimal support. The chronic lack of publicly subsidised childcare, in particular, has tended to confine British mothers to being secondary earners if partnered, and low/no earners if not, as discussed more fully in Chapter Four. Falling fertility rates, which reflect women's difficulties in reconciling motherhood with increasing employment participation (Duncan, 2002), are a major cause of ageing populations. Achieving the policy goal of promoting women's employment and independent pension entitlements without further depressing fertility rates – an outcome important to the sustainability of pension schemes – is considered in Chapter Six, in the context of policies in other EU countries.

British women's difficulties in accommodating the dual roles of paid and unpaid work are central to understanding the persistence of the gender gap in hours of employment and earnings. These gender inequalities in the labour market, which lead to women's lower pension income in later life, are described in the next section.

Gender inequalities in employment

British men and women's overall rates of participation in the labour market are converging. While the economic activity rate of working-age men (16-64) declined from 94 to 79% between 1959 and 2000, that of working-age women (16-59) rose from 47 to 70% over the same period (ONS, 2002b, Chart 4.1). However, much of the increase in women's employment is in part-time work. In 2001, 37% of working-age women were employed full time and 28% part time. The corresponding figures for men were 61% and 5% (ONS, 2002b). The proportions of men and women who were full- and part-time employees in 1986 and 2001 are shown in Figure 1.3. Women's full-time employment grew noticeably between 1986 and 1990 but there has been no increase between 1990 and 2001.

Thus the gender convergence in employment participation is deceptive: full-time employment of women remains much lower than men's and may have stalled at under 40%, severely limiting women's earnings and ability to build an adequate pension income.

Two factors magnify the effect of the gender differences in full-time employment rates on lifetime earnings. First, women's age profile of employment participation differs from men's. British women's full-time employment rates tend to peak in their twenties, when relatively few have had children, and in their forties, reflecting women's return to longer hours of employment as children become more independent (see Figure 1.4). The timing in the lifecourse of part-time working is relevant to occupational status achieved and to earnings. Among women, part-time work is common in the prime earning years between ages 30-54 (Figure 1.4) when opportunities for wage gains and advancement would otherwise be highest. In contrast, part-time work among men is rare under age 55.

Second, the combination of this age profile with the characteristics of part-time jobs in Britain undermines women's capacity to earn pension entitlements.

Figure 1.3: Percentage employed, by employment status, men and women aged 16-64 (1986 and 2001)

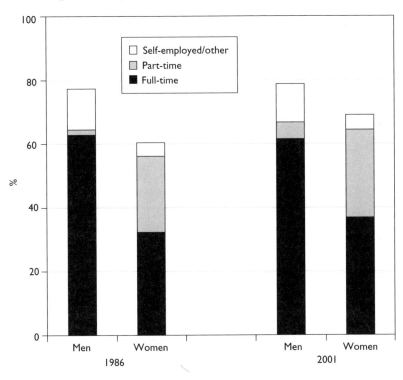

Note: As % of population aged 16-64.
Source: ONS (2002b, Table 4.3)

Part-time work is generally associated with poorer working conditions, job insecurity, lack of training and career development opportunities and lack of fringe benefits, as well as lower hourly pay. Part-time workers are typically concentrated in small firms, in certain private sector industries which are highly feminised and poorly unionised – all contributing to low pay (Paci et al, 1995). The effects of part-time work tend to be long-lasting and may apply even to well-qualified women. Qualitative research on British women who entered the labour market between 1946 and 1970 showed that the adverse effect of part-time employment on mothers' occupational status (relative to mothers employed full time) applied equally to earlier and later birth cohorts of women, despite the better qualifications held by later cohorts (Jacobs, 1999).

There has been a growth in the proportion of 'short' part-time jobs (under 20 hours per week) in Britain; such jobs tend to be of very poor quality and to act as a trap rather than a bridge to a better job. The EU Social Chapter obliges member states to set minimum hourly wages (although these are still very low)

Figure 1.4: Percentage of women employed full and part time by age group

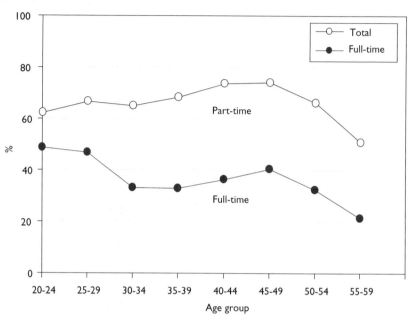

Note: Full-time employment defined as 31+ hours.

Source: Ginn et al (2001, Figure 2.2), using data from the GHS 1993-94

and to ensure part-timers have equal access with full-timers to maternity leave, career break schemes, sick leave and redundancy pay. Britain enacted the necessary legislation in 2000. Some improvements for part-timers can be expected, although it takes time for the effects of legislation to translate into employment practices.

Women's gaps in employment, or reduction in hours of paid work, after giving birth are greater in Britain than in those European countries where affordable quality childcare services are widely available (Joshi and Davies, 1992). Women's maternal and marital status also affects their likelihood of being employed full time (as discussed more fully in Chapter Four).

Gender inequalities in earnings

Since contributions to private pensions are based on earnings, higher earnings over a longer period generally translate into higher pensions, although the precise relationship depends on the type of pension scheme. In final salary occupational pension schemes, earnings after age 40 are especially important to the amount of pension entitlement, as the latter is based on salary in the last few years before retirement, as well as on years of membership. In defined contribution (DC) schemes, contributions are invested on the stock market, building a fund that is annuitised at or soon after retirement. In such schemes, the individual bears the risks of both poor investment choices by the plan provider and of adverse developments on world stock markets as a whole. The fund accumulated at retirement reflects the level and duration of contributions but also the time they have had to grow. Thus contributions made early in the working life are most important. DC pension schemes may be occupational or personal (including stakeholder) pensions.

Among all full-time British employees, women's hourly earnings are still only 82% of men's, and among non-manual employees even lower at 70%. Hourly earnings of women employed part time are lower still, only 61% of the hourly earnings of men employed full time (ONS, 2001). Even among full-timers, women tend to work shorter hours than men and their weekly pay was 74% of men's in 1999 (Rake et al, 2000). The earnings of married women, in particular, remain far below men's, both nationally and within couples (Arber and Ginn, 1995). A fifth of employed women work less than eight hours per week, most earning wages too low to allow contributions to either state or private pensions. Those who are low paid tend to remain low paid and there is a high turnover between low pay and non-employment (McKnight et al, 1998). Toynbee (2003) blames women's low pay on the low level of the Minimum Wage (£4.20 per hour in 2002-03) and on the continuing low valuation of what are regarded as women's skills – caring, cleaning, cooking, teaching and nursing. Pay in these occupations is falling further behind that of male-dominated occupations.

The gender gap in pay is modified by factors such as women's lifecourse stage, family circumstances, educational level, occupational class and ethnicity. Recognising this diversity is crucial to understanding variation in the extent of women's pension disadvantage relative to men. For example, whereas men's earnings tend to rise with age, suggesting they receive a premium for age and experience, women's earnings decline from age 30, reflecting their interrupted employment patterns and labour market segmentation. For workers in their twenties, the gender gap in full-time hourly wages has diminished since 1976 from about 15% to less than 10%. But the gender gap widens after age 30 and is around 25% among all those aged over 40 (Rake et al, 2000, p 46-7). Figure 1.5 shows the gender gap in individual income by age group during the working life. The widening of the gender pay gap with age is likely to reflect the cumulative effects of women's involvement in family caring work and also gendered ageism, in which employers perceive women employees as too old for training or promotion at a younger age than equivalent men (Itzin and Phillipson, 1993).

Family responsibilities and especially motherhood magnify the gender pay gap. The 'family gap in pay' – or the wage loss due to the presence of dependent children – for women aged 24-44, after taking account of age, education and other relevant variables, was relatively large in Britain compared with other countries, rising from 8% for one child to 24% for two children (Harkness and Waldfogel, 1999).

Figure 1.5: Median individual income of men and women by age group

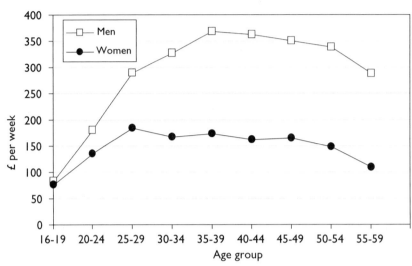

Source: ONS (2002b, adapted from Chart 5.5), data for 1999

The gender pay gap may diminish for later cohorts, as younger women enter the labour market with better educational qualifications and benefit from improved labour market opportunities. However, neither qualifications nor entry to top occupations guarantee gender equality in pay. Indeed, economists have shown that gender inequality in earnings widens with occupational status and that the relationship between occupational status and earnings is weaker for women than for men in Britain (Sloane, 1990).

The extent to which periods of caring for children or older relatives place women at a disadvantage in acquiring pension entitlements of their own depends on the structure of the pension system, including the balance of public and private provision and redistributive features in state pension schemes. In the next section, gender-relevant features and reforms in the British pension system are examined.

Gender and the changing British pension system

The design of British welfare institutions incorporated the assumption that women would either marry and have financial support throughout their life from a husband, or would remain single and childless, pursuing a career in the same way as men (Lister, 1994). State pensions have since been modified to reflect changes in gender relations, but the declining value of state pensions and the increasingly heavy reliance on private pensions has rendered these adaptations ineffective in ensuring women's economic independence in later life. The gender effects of pension policy since 1980 can be seen in the changing ratio of older women's income to older men's. In the mid-1980s older women's median personal income was 71% of men's, declining to 62% in 1993-94 and only 53% in 1998. Women have been less able than men to compensate for declining state pensions through private sector pensions.

Women in Britain, if they marry, can obtain retirement income through three main routes, which are conceptually distinct although often combined in practice. These are:

1. sharing a husband's pension income;
2. receiving pensions derived from a husband's (or former husband's) pension contributions (as wives, ex-wives or widows); and
3. receiving pensions based on their own contributions.

Relying on the first route is a risky strategy. First, an increasing proportion of marriages end in divorce and divorced women are unlikely to obtain an adequate pension settlement, as discussed in Chapter Four. Second, not all husbands share their pension income equally. Third, husbands are not necessarily successful breadwinners and pension earners, especially if they suffer redundancy or ill-health in midlife, curtailing their pension-earning years. The second route, through pensions derived from a husband's contributions to pension schemes, has the drawback that such pensions are often small. Most marriages end in widowhood for the woman – about half of British women aged over 65 are widows. Widows generally receive only half their deceased husband's occupational pension and may receive a smaller fraction from his personal pension. The third route, in which women acquire pension entitlements based on their own employment, can provide financial security but this is only possible in a women-friendly pension system – one that minimises the pension effects of gaps in employment and periods of low earnings due to caring commitments. A primary concern of this book is to explore to what extent women are able to build adequate state and private pensions of their own – the 'independence model' of pensions – and how pension policy promotes or frustrates this outcome.

Because current older women's incomes reflect pension policies in place up to 50 years ago, it is helpful to set out the main changes in pension structure, focusing on gender effects and distinguishing three policy periods between 1940 and 2002: establishment of state and private pension schemes (1940-74); revitalising state pensions (1975-80); and state pension retrenchment with promotion of private pensions (1980 on).

State pensions 1940-74

The retirement pension introduced by the 1946 National Insurance Act was originally intended to be "sufficient without further resources to provide the minimum income needed for subsistence" (Beveridge, 1942, p 122), although low enough to encourage voluntary additional saving by breadwinners, mainly men. However, Beveridge's 'subsistence' amounts were not based on objective study of need and were more miserly than Rowntree's 'primary poverty' standard. Compared with social insurance contribution levels in other EU countries, Britain's National Insurance (NI) contributions are relatively low. This is reflected in state spending on individuals aged over 55, which is over 10% of GDP on average for the EU but only 5.5% in Britain (EPC, 2001).

Because of the gendered assumptions on which the welfare state was based, a married man's NI contributions buy a basic flat-rate pension for two – his own and a reduced (60%) Category B pension. This is payable for a wife when she is over state pension age (60, but rising to 65 by 2020) provided her husband is aged at least 65. This arrangement gives rise to the inequity that a wife who earns entitlements in her own right through paying NI contributions may receive no more than a stay-at-home wife, even though both may have had similar domestic responsibilities. Widows over state pension age receive a basic pension equal to their deceased husband's (if better than their own entitlement) and divorced women can use their ex-husband's contribution record for the period of the marriage if this improves their own entitlement. Thus the post-war welfare state 'compensates' married women for limited opportunities in the labour market through derived benefits – that is, benefits based on their husband's contributions.

Women's lower state pension age of 60, compared with 65 for men, was conceded in 1940 following representations from the National Spinsters' Association and from married men whose wives were several years younger than themselves and therefore ineligible for the Category B pension at the time the husband reached age 65 (Thane, 1978). This reform was deemed a cheaper solution than increasing the level of the basic pension.

In most other respects, women were ill-served by the Beveridge scheme. Married women were handicapped by the notorious 'half test', whereby those paying contributions for less than half their working life since marriage lost the value of *all* their contributions. Periods of caring for children, parents or parents-in-law attracted no credits in the basic pension. Married women were further discouraged from building their own pension by the right to opt for reduced National Insurance (NI) contributions which carried no pension entitlement – the Married Woman's Exemption, or 'small stamp'. Many married women did not appreciate that paying a reduced NI contribution disqualified them from receiving a basic state pension of their own. As a result of these gender-biased provisions and women's short employment records, only a quarter of women pensioners in the late 1990s received a basic pension solely through their own contributions and of these only half received the full amount. A further third were married women with a Category B (60%) pension and just over 40% were widows with a Category B (100%) pension (Social Security Committee, 2000, p 168).

The value of the pension increased slightly, as a proportion of male manual earnings, from 19.1% in 1948 to 21.5% in 1975 (Johnson and Falkingham, 1992), yet for most of the post-war period it has remained about 10% below the level of means-tested benefits and thus wholly inadequate to live on. From

1961, a small state Graduated Pension was introduced. This extended an earnings-related scheme to those excluded from occupational pensions, but was too little and too late to stem the demand for private provision (Hannah, 1986).

Private pensions 1940-74

The low level of state pensions fostered rapid expansion in occupational pension coverage from only 13% of the workforce in 1936 to 47% in 1967, falling slightly to 46% in the 1970s (Hannah, 1986). While other European states provided substantial state earnings-related pension schemes to most employees, Beveridge's recommendations had "furthered the conditions within social security for the growth of a multi-billion-pound enterprise of private pensions" (Shragge, 1984, p 33). When the Graduated Pension was introduced, occupational pensions meeting certain standards were allowed to contract out, diverting the increase in National Insurance contributions of both employer and employee into the private scheme. The lack of a realistic state second tier pension and the growing importance of occupational pensions were to have serious consequences for British employed women, because of their limited access to occupational pensions.

Most occupational pension schemes provide a defined benefit (DB) pension at retirement, based on the individual's years of pension scheme membership and final salary (their average salary in the final few years before retirement). The extra contributions generally made by employers to their occupational pension schemes, above the minimum required to replace the state second tier pension, are effectively a form of deferred wages and make occupational pensions a valuable fringe benefit of employment. British employers' welfare payments, as a proportion of total employee remuneration, doubled between the mid-1960s and the 1980s (Green et al, 1984), improving benefits for the minority of the population belonging to an occupational pension scheme but exacerbating the social division of welfare (Titmuss, 1958). The social cleavage was of gender as well as class, with women's coverage by private pensions well below men's. A major reason is that part-time employees were often excluded from occupational pension schemes. This has been unlawful in the EU since 1986 (following the Bilka-Kaufhaus judgment) and in Britain the 1995 Pensions Act prohibited the exclusion of part-timers from occupational pension schemes. However, small employers in the private sector, for whom women part-timers often work, rarely operate an occupational pension scheme (Ginn and Arber, 1993).

The return on contributions in an occupational pension scheme is greatest for those with continuous membership until retirement and earnings that rise with age. Those who leave the scheme early, mainly women with family responsibilities, receive less value for their contributions. Also, women tend to have a flatter earnings profile than men, with a lower final salary and hence a lower pension even for the minority of women whose length of service matches men's. Thus women have both lower coverage rates than men and poorer benefits due to lower earnings, fewer pensionable years and the penalties of early leaving (Groves, 1987; Ginn and Arber, 1991, 1993, 1996). Despite being hailed as a success story, occupational schemes have yielded quite modest pensions. Among the recently retired with an occupational pension, the median amount for a non-married man in 2000 was £81 per week and even less for a comparable woman: £47 per week (House of Commons, 2002).

It was not until 1975 that a Labour government introduced a radical new state pension scheme, which addressed a number of the inadequacies of state pension provision and promised a much better pensions deal for women.

Revitalising state pensions 1975-80

The 1975 Social Security Benefits Act introduced by Labour heralded major improvements to the British state pension system. First, the basic pension was formally indexed to rises in national earnings or prices, whichever was the higher. This ensured that older people would share in rising national prosperity and signalled that the basic pension would provide a secure foundation on which individuals could build other sources of income in later life. Second, the pension needs of women were explicitly addressed for the first time. The 'half test' was abolished and the Married Woman's Exemption phased out. Although married women who were already paying reduced NI contributions were allowed to continue after 1978, women who divorced were required to pay the full stamp. Most important, Home Responsibilities Protection (HRP) allowed years of family caring to count towards eligibility for the basic state pension. Those not in paid employment or who earn less than the Lower Earnings Limit (LEL) (about £75 per week in 2002), are excluded from contributing to the NI system. This applies to some two million women each year (McKnight et al, 1998). However, if they are caring for a child aged under 16 (or 18 if in full-time education) they qualify automatically for HRP. Carers of a frail or disabled adult may also be covered by HRP. HRP reduces the number of contribution years required for entitlement to the basic pension so that, provided NI contributions have been paid for at least 20 years, a woman may still qualify for the full amount if the remaining years are covered by HRP. It was expected that pensioners would increasingly be floated off means-tested benefits by a rising basic pension and that HRP would eventually ensure that most women would receive the full amount in their own right. By protecting pension rights during caring years, HRP promised to help accommodate women's dual commitments to family and employment.

A new State Earnings-Related Pension Scheme (SERPS) replaced the meagre Graduated Pension. Benefits, based on the best 20 years of earnings (revalued at state pension age), would accrue at 1.25% per annum and entitlements were automatically portable across jobs or across gaps in employment – a great advantage for those with interrupted employment patterns, particularly women. Contributions to SERPS through the NI scheme were compulsory for all employees earning above the LEL, unless they contracted out into an occupational pension scheme.

The new state pension package, if allowed to mature, would have been redistributive towards the low paid, as well as minimising the adverse effect of women's caring responsibilities on their state pension income. A woman on average female manual earnings could expect (at maturity of SERPS in 1998) a replacement rate of 50% of her earnings from the combination of basic pension and SERPS, while her higher paid non-manual sister could have expected a replacement rate of 43% (Groves, 1991). The benefits of the 1975 legislation were shared across generations, helping both current pensioners and working-age people. The reinvigoration of state pensions was short-lived, however, overtaken by the neo-liberal reforms of the 1980s.

Retrenchment of state pensions 1980-2002

With the election of a Conservative government in 1979, an individualistic, competitive ideology gained ascendancy, expressed in privatisation of many aspects of welfare. The ensuing spate of reforms included cutting state pensions and promoting private personal pensions as an alternative to SERPS, a policy that ignored women's lesser ability to acquire private pensions. The main changes since 1980 are briefly outlined.

From 1980, the basic state pension has been indexed only to prices, eroding its relative value from 20% of average male earnings in 1980 to around 15% in 2002. It is projected to decline to only 7% by 2050 (DSS, 1998), falling ever further below the level of means-tested benefits.

The second tier SERPS was scaled back in the 1986 Social Security Act, so that it would in future provide a maximum pension of 20% (instead of 25%) of revalued earnings. A major change was that the pension was to be based on average earnings over a working life of 44 years for women and 49 years for men, instead of average over the best 20 years. This substantially reduces the amount of SERPS pension for those with periods out of employment or on low earnings, compared with the original formula that would have become mature in 1998. There was a further cut in SERPS for women. Those widowed after October 2002 will inherit only half their deceased husband's SERPS, instead of the whole amount as originally provided in the 1975 Act.

The 1995 Pensions Act brought yet another cut to state pensions in the future, affecting women only. Their state pension age will be raised from 60 to 65, phasing in the change from 2010 until 2020. By 2020, women will need 44 years of contributions instead of 39 (including any HRP years) to qualify for a full basic pension. Similarly, for the state second tier pension, average earnings over 49 instead of 44 years will be used to calculate the pension entitlement. These changes will substantially reduce the amount of state pension income for women born after 1950, unless they are able to continue in full-time employment until age 65 (Hutton et al, 1995).

In 2002, SERPS was replaced by the State Second Pension (S2P). This differs from SERPS in two ways. First, it will provide a higher pension for the low paid than SERPS, by applying a higher accrual rate to low earnings bands.

Second, there is some carer protection in S2P, in that mothers of a child up to age six are credited into the scheme as if they were paying contributions on earnings of about £10,000 pa. Some of those caring for adults may also qualify for carer credits. It is planned that the S2P will become a flat-rate pension by 2007. These reforms potentially benefit women. However, because of the projected decline in value of the basic pension under current policy, the S2P and basic pension combined will only provide a pension below the level at which means-tested benefits are payable (Falkingham and Rake, 2001; Brooks et al, 2002; Falkingham et al, 2002). Thus "the new State Second Pension will make little difference to women as the gains from this will be washed out by the ongoing erosion of the basic state pension" (Evason and Spence, 2002, p 4). The low level of the combined basic and S2P perpetuates the pensions poverty trap, in which additional pensions, savings or earnings may bring no financial gain because of the loss of means-tested benefits.

An indication of the extent of state pension cuts planned by the Labour government in 1998 is provided by projections to 2050. The cost of the state pensions (basic and SERPS/S2P) was projected to fall from £34bn to £26bn (in 1997 earnings terms) and the value of the combined state pensions to fall from 37 to 20% of average male earnings in 2050 (PPG, 1998). Spending on state pensions was projected to fall from 4.4 to 3.4% of GDP (DSS, 1998). Above-inflation rises in the basic pension in 2001 (+7.4%) and 2002 (+4.1%) slightly modify these projections. The government hoped that the shortfall in older people's incomes would be met by a further expansion of private pensions; their aim was to reverse the balance of pension provision, which was then 60% state and 40% private.

Expansion of private pensions 1980-2002

Despite warnings from the government's natural supporters as early as 1985 that personal pensions would bring poorer returns for many employees than SERPS (for example, CBI, 1985), the Conservative government pressed ahead, providing generous financial incentives to encourage individuals to opt out of SERPS into the new Appropriate Personal Pensions. These personal pensions are individual portable defined contribution (DC) accounts whose fund must be annuitised (converted to an annual income for life) at or during retirement. A major drawback, played down at that time, is that investment risk is individualised, shared neither with the workforce as a whole nor even with members of an employer's scheme. Some five million individuals took the bait, providing lucrative business for the personal pensions industry but dubious benefits to contributors. Some companies set up group pension schemes on a DC basis, reducing administration costs and sharing investment risk among a larger group.

Personal pensions provide poor value for most women and for the low paid (Davies and Ward, 1992; Waine, 1995; Ginn and Arber, 2000a). In any DC scheme, contributions made early in the working life have a disproportionate effect on the fund at retirement; yet women's ability to contribute is often very limited until their children have become independent. To make matters worse, the same size of fund buys an annuity for a woman that is about 10% less than a man's, due to actuarial calculations reflecting women's greater average longevity. The charging structure, with flat-rate fees paid predominantly in the first year of membership, penalises the low paid and those with breaks in contributions, making personal pensions a very poor option for women who have gaps in full-time employment when their children are young. Charges for administration, investment management and annuitisation may reduce the value of contributions by 45%, according to experts (Murthi et al, 2001). An estimated 30-40% of personal pension account holders find that charges actually exceed the amount they have contributed (Disney and Johnson, 1997). Many employees succumbed to high-pressure sales techniques and opted out of an advantageous occupational pension scheme into a personal pension – the mis-selling scandal (Ward, 1996). The issue of proliferating pension choices and new risks is considered more fully in Chapter Two.

Stakeholder pensions (SHPs) were introduced in 2001 partly as a result of the tarnished image of personal pensions. Employers with over five employees who do not operate an approved occupational pension scheme are required to offer an SHP to their employees. SHPs are a more heavily regulated form of personal pension, provided by the same companies that provide personal pensions but intended for individuals with modest to average incomes. SHPs have the advantage of a cap on administration charges at 1% per annum of the fund and a feature which is particularly helpful to women is that gaps in SHP contributions incur no extra charges. Contributions of up to £3,600 per annum can be made to an SHP on behalf of a non-earner. However, this will only help women with a husband (or other relative) who is well-off, generous and accepts women's need for their own independent pension entitlement. Drawbacks are that SHPs share with other personal pensions the risk of poor investment returns. Moreover, hidden fees (such as dealing charges) are not capped so that costs may still be high relative to individuals' contributions (Wynn, 2001). If the S2P becomes flat-rate by 2007 as planned, SHPs will be the only earnings-related pensions available for the moderately paid who lack access to an occupational pension.

The policy of encouraging contracting out of state second tier pensions through advantageous rebates is costly, withdrawing financial resources from the National Insurance (NI) system and hence reducing the scope to improve the state pensions that are the mainstay of older women's income. Although the Conservative government claimed that opting out of SERPS would reduce public spending, the net cost of the financial incentives to opt out, from 1988 to 1993, was estimated as £6,000 million (1988 prices) (NAO, 1990). Every pound paid in rebate on a personal pension incurs a net cost to the NI Fund of 22p (PPG, 1998) and this subsidy applies equally to SHPs.

A further loss of public resources that is largely invisible arises from tax relief on private (occupational and personal) pension contributions by employees and employers. Tax relief on private pensions is long-standing but the amount of tax lost in this way grew dramatically under the Thatcher administration, from £1.2 billion in 1979 to £8.2 billion in 1991 (Wilkinson, 1993), reflecting the spread of personal pensions, and continued to rise (Sinfield, 2000). By 2000 such tax spending (not counting the £1.5-2.2 billion tax forgone on lump sums from pension schemes) had risen to £13.7 billion in that year, equivalent to over 40% of state spending on the basic NI pension (Sinfield, 2000). Tax spending on private pension incentives is highly regressive, with half the benefit received by the top 10% of taxpayers and a quarter by the top 2.5% (Agulnik and Le Grand, 1998). Pensions tax relief and rebates cost Britain nearly 3% of GDP in forgone revenue (Adema, 2000), a huge expenditure that could otherwise be spent on improved state pensions. A gender audit of tax spending has not been carried out but it is likely that men are the chief beneficiaries, while women have been harder hit than men by the cutbacks in state pensions.

The main elements of the British pension system in 2002 are shown diagrammatically in Figure 1.6. For a comprehensive account, focusing on the relationship between state and private pensions, see Liu (1999). Employees must make NI contributions to both the basic state pension and a second tier pension, but may choose to contract out of S2P into one of a variety of private schemes, including occupational and personal pensions. However, the choices are more limited for those lacking access to an occupational pension scheme. As noted above, final salary occupational pension schemes (DB) are the most advantageous, due to the employer's contribution, which is generally higher

Figure 1.6: Outline structure of the British pension regime (2002)

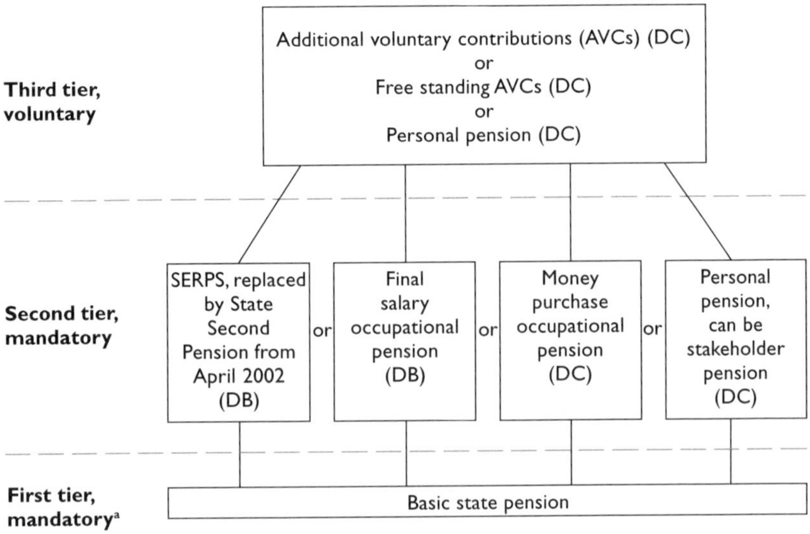

Note:[a] Those earning below the Lower Earnings Limit (LEL) pay no National Insurance contributions, but may acquire credits through Home Responsibilities Protection; those earning between the LEL and the Lower Earnings Threshold (LET) acquire NI credits; those earning above the LET must pay NI contributions. For the self-employed, second tier pensions are not compulsory.

than in an occupational money purchase (DC) or personal pension scheme. Those with sufficient income may opt to make additional voluntary contributions (AVCs) to an individually arranged personal pension, to a company-sponsored AVC scheme or to an individually arranged free standing AVC.

Analysts from academic, political and actuarial backgrounds have questioned whether the government's pension policy is politically sustainable. In the final chapter, the major concerns expressed – about pensioner poverty, savings disincentives due to means-testing and failures in the private pensions sector – are considered, along with policy alternatives.

Summary

This chapter has outlined British trends in gender relations and in women's employment and earnings, tracing the parallel changes in the pension system that will influence gender differences in pension income in the future.

The remainder of the book is organised as follows. Chapter Two is concerned with pension choices and analyses gender and class inequalities in the ability to contribute to the expanding range of types of private pension, using data from the General Household Survey (GHS). The characteristics of employees who have opted for personal pensions or remained in the state pension scheme are examined, distinguishing between those with access to an occupational pension and those without, and considering the implications for later life income.

Little is known about the pension prospects of men and women from minority ethnic groups and how they are affected by disadvantage and discrimination in the labour market, as well as different cultural norms concerning women's employment. Chapter Three uses data from the Family Resources Survey to analyse variation in employment and private pension scheme membership according to gender and specific ethnic group.

Chapter Four examines how the impact of childrearing on participation in paid employment and private pension scheme membership differs according to women's partnership status, using data from the GHS. Recent legislation permitting pension sharing is considered in relation to the pension needs of divorced and cohabiting men and women.

Chapter Five also uses GHS data, focusing on differentiation among women in their employment and private pension coverage, according to their educational qualifications. It critically examines the thesis that graduate mothers can largely avoid the adverse impact of childrearing on future pension income, in contrast to less skilled women.

Chapter Six turns to the European Union, comparing trends in fertility and women's employment, and the differing extent to which EU pension systems are adequate and adapted to the needs of those with caring commitments.

Finally, Chapter Seven summarises the gender implications of British pension policy, examines the concerns of a range of critics and discusses the main alternative strategies proposed, focusing on the gender implications of each.

TWO

Choice and risk in pensions: gender and class inequalities

Pension providers and governments alike warn that individuals need to save more through private pensions. Most economists attribute lack of saving to irrational behaviour described as 'myopia' – an inappropriately short time horizon. Yet individuals often have sound reasons for reluctance to save additional amounts towards pensions (Rowlingson, 2002). These include a rational response to uncertainties, especially the risk of a poor return on investments. The mis-selling of personal pensions and the theft and misuse of occupational funds are indications of the way pension risks and costs are increasingly passed on to individuals (Ward, 1996; Peggs, 2000; Ring, 2002). Meanwhile state pensions are shrinking as governments seek to reduce state spending on pensions, as part of a more general rolling back of the welfare state (Aldridge, 1998). Confronted with unsatisfactory state pensions and risky private provision, even individuals who can afford to are understandably reluctant to save for their old age in this way.

Widening choice, growing complexity and uncertainty about the future of pensions means an increasing risk of making decisions that do not provide the best value for money. When politicians and pensions experts admit they find the British pension system hard to grasp, it is no wonder that individuals are bemused by pension scheme rules, and that many feel alienated or misled by 'information' from the state or the purveyors of private pensions. For those with interrupted and unpredictable employment trajectories, choosing an optimal pension strategy becomes well-nigh impossible.

This chapter first considers the issue of pension choice in the context of uncertainty about risks in the various types of second tier pensions. Gender and class inequalities in pension coverage are then analysed using data from the General Household Survey (GHS). The characteristics of employees who opted for a personal pension or who remained in the state pension scheme are examined, distinguishing between those who could have belonged to an occupational pension and those who lacked access to such a scheme. The chapter finally considers the issue of mis-selling of personal pension plans to men and women for whom this was unlikely to be the best option.

Choice, information and risk

Pension choices were limited during the post-war period before the 1980s. Where employers offered an occupational pension scheme, membership was compulsory. The main social divisions were between employees with or without an occupational pension scheme (although the quality of these varied) and between employees and the self-employed. For most employees, individual advice was not important; information about pensions, such as from a trade union or employer, would apply to most of a company's employees. However, married women's long-standing right to opt for the 'small stamp' in National Insurance led to many making a decision they regretted at retirement, having not realised that they would forfeit a basic state pension in their own right. This exemplifies the 'downside' of choice.

Choices in pensions have proliferated since the 1980s. Pension saving in the first and second tiers of pension is compulsory for most workers (see Chapter One, Figure 1.6), with a number of options – whether to contract out of the state scheme into an occupational or personal pension, whether to make additional contributions above the compulsory level, whether to invest any surplus income into housing or other forms of saving or whether to use all income for immediate needs. Decision making is beset by multiple unpredictabilities. These include not only the future performance of the stock market as a whole, of specific pensions and savings plans and of the housing market, but also the individual's future employment, earnings trajectory, retirement timing and family circumstances.

Pension choices are made in the context of an ideological and moral climate constructed by policy makers, commercial interests and the media. Since the mid-1980s, Conservative governments engaged in a 'rhetoric of responsibility' (Smart, 1999) in which contributing to a private pension was portrayed as responsible behaviour while paying into state pensions was not. This ideological position, which is in sharp contrast to the rest of Europe, was associated with an emphasis on consumer power and choice, the latter being linked to notions of good and evil and right and wrong (Phillips, 1998). The morally inferior status assigned by this rhetorical framing to those relying solely on state pensions affects mainly older women (see Chapter One). Such dependence on state pensions may seem to disqualify recipients from full citizenship. It "withdraws their status as adults [and] may promote the insidious idea that, like children in Victorian Britain, they may be seen but not heard" (Mann, 2001, p 138). The potentially disempowering effects of social disapproval are magnified for those older people who depend on means-tested benefits, again mainly women. The Labour government elected in 1997, despite having condemned Conservative pensions policy while in opposition, continues to imply that making provision for retirement income through the private sector is morally superior, encouraging individuals to contract out of the state second tier pension through financial incentives (see Chapter One).

People's understanding of second-tier pension schemes is limited (Williams and Field, 1993). Occupational pensions are often taken up without much forethought or knowledge and the complexity of written material about pension schemes is a deterrent (Field and Farrant, 1993). Contributors to personal pensions similarly lack understanding about them (Williams and Field, 1993) and advice about the implications of women's interrupted employment patterns has been lacking (Davies and Ward, 1992).

Women are particularly prone to feel uninformed about pensions. Hawkes and Garman (1995) found that women were three times more likely than men to say they had not joined an available occupational pension scheme because they knew too little about pensions or had not given enough thought to the matter. Almost 40% of contributors to a personal pension thought they would receive a guaranteed amount, unaware that their pension was linked to stock market performance. Employees also lacked understanding about the State Earnings-Related Pension Scheme (SERPS). Thus 42% of full-time employees who were not contracted out into a private pension scheme thought they were not contributing to SERPS, despite this being the default option (Hawkes and Garman, 1995).

With an increasing range of options, especially the introduction of personal pensions in 1988, the chance of making substantial losses due to a particular pension decision has escalated. Large numbers of people, against their best interests, opted out of sound occupational pension schemes into a personal pension which was likely to provide a lower pension – "a clear case of poorly-informed buyers confronted with sales staff with a powerful incentive to sell" (Mann, 2001, p 133). This mis-selling scandal, with compensation to investors estimated to cost £13.5 billion (Jones, 2000) and the high-profile fraud of Robert Maxwell that robbed Mirror Group employees of their occupational pension fund, began to reveal the shaky nature of the pensions promise offered by private sector providers. Investigations revealed multiple flaws (Goode, 1993), and prompted a search, which does not seem to have been very successful, for regulatory mechanisms to prevent a repetition and restore confidence.

Neither the endemic nature of private pension risk nor the inability of experts to provide advice to protect against such risk was fully appreciated by the public in the early 1990s. Despite a proliferation of regulatory bodies concerned with the conduct of the private pensions industry, the increased speed of trading stocks, with globalisation of finance markets and computerised processing, have all reduced the feasibility of regulation (Mann, 2001). Because pension funds occupy a grey area in terms of ownership, fund managers are enabled to act primarily in the interests of their shareholders, producing a poor deal for pension scheme members (Blackburn, 2002). In Britain, the collapse of Equitable Life's guarantees after 1999 showed that even an ancient and respected institution (founded in 1762) can make mistakes, while the implosion of Enron in the US in 2002 demonstrated (if this were necessary) that neither the integrity of top executives nor the independence of auditors can be assumed. These events highlight the irrelevance of financial education of consumers in the face of boardroom incompetence or fraud.

Warnings about the effect of ageing populations on the future sustainability of state Pay-As-You-Go pension schemes have been rife but the equivalent threat to the viability of private funded pensions has been largely ignored. Indeed, a persuasive message of governments and private pension providers has been that a personal pension fund is inviolate, owned and controlled by the contributor. The risk of loss in value was downplayed and despite the mantra (in small print) that share prices can go down as well as up, few took this warning seriously during the bull market of the late 1980s and early 1990s. Those belonging to occupational pension schemes were also blissfully unaware of the level of risk until the trickle of closures and reductions in projected benefits became a river in 2002 (see Chapter Seven).

Shock at the pensions crisis might have been less if debate on pension privatisation in the 1980s and 1990s had been more balanced. Challenging the dominant expert discourse and assumptions has been less evident in pensions than in medicine and law, enabling fund managers, actuaries and advisers to marginalise the voices of pensioners and contributing members (Mann, 2001). Policy makers have failed to take seriously the arguments for maintaining robust state pension provision. The only organised resistance to the creeping individualisation of risk in pensions has come from the trade unions, first in successfully demanding a larger rise in the basic pension at the 2000 Labour Party conference and more recently in arguing for protection of final salary occupational pension rights and for employers who operate an occupational pension scheme to be compelled to contribute 10% of payroll (TUC, 2002). This latter proposal could, however, increase the stampede away from occupational pensions, leaving most employees with a choice between a stakeholder pension and the State Second Pension.

The reductions in state pensions outlined in Chapter One – the decline in value of the basic pensions, numerous cuts in SERPS and a rising state pension age – are a collective loss imposed initially by Conservative governments in the 1980s and 1990s. Private pension losses are more likely to be experienced as a personal misfortune or as resulting from a failure of the individual's financial judgement. The idea that each individual is responsible for pension decisions that turned out badly is reinforced by the calls for increased financial education, implying that if individuals had been better informed they could have avoided or minimised their loss. This is true only in the sense that resistance to pension privatisation might have been more widespread had the voting public realised the risks; but having been hustled onto the *Titanic* of pension privatisation, with inadequate state pension lifeboats, few could avoid the disaster entirely.

The emphasis on pension choices and financial education not only facilitates blaming the victims but also ignores the fact that vulnerable social groups have less advantageous choices available to them. This applies particularly to women. Due to the low level of the basic state pension and the brief time in which SERPS has operated, private pensions are a major source of gender and class inequality of retirement income (Arber and Ginn, 1991; Ginn and Arber, 1991, 1999). This is increasingly so as the basic pension declines, reducing its redistributive effects. The next section examines gender differences in private pension coverage, among those of working age.

The gender gap in private pensions

The gender difference in private pension coverage among employees is stark, mainly because a higher proportion of women work part time. The reason for low membership of occupational pension schemes among part-timers differs according to the sector of industry (Ginn and Arber, 1993). Women employed part time in the private sector tend to work for an employer who does not operate a scheme; in 1987, 71% of women part-timers in this sector gave this as their reason for not belonging to an occupational pension scheme and part-timers are still concentrated in jobs where no occupational pension scheme is offered. In the public sector, where such schemes are more common, it was legal in the past for an occupational pension scheme's rules to exclude part-timers from membership. In 1987, 44% of women part-timers working in the public sector who were not members gave this as their reason (Ginn and Arber, 1993). European Court judgments deeming exclusion of part-timers to be indirect discrimination against women had some effect and in Britain it has been illegal since 1995 to discriminate against part-time employees in terms of access to occupational pensions. In 1995, 30% of British occupational pension schemes in the private sector of industry and 8% in the public sector still excluded some part-timers, the hours limit for eligibility varying among schemes (NAPF, 1996). Part-timers' occupational pension coverage has since increased. While this may help women in the future, many midlife and older women have lost the chance of accruing occupational pension entitlements for those periods of the lifecourse when they worked part time to accommodate the demands of childrearing.

Even when women do join an occupational pension scheme they tend to derive less benefit from it than men for several reasons. First, many women leave their employment and hence the pension scheme for family reasons, long before normal retirement age. Their pension rights may then be 'preserved' in the scheme for later payment. Although a degree of inflation proofing is now required for preserved pensions, the entitlement will be much less than if the member had remained in the scheme and benefited from the rise in earnings. A large minority of early leavers receive no pension at all, having withdrawn their own contributions after one or two years' membership and forfeited the value of their employer's contributions. Thus over 30% of women aged 60-74 in 1994 who had joined an occupational pension were never able to draw a pension from it, compared to only 14% of men (Disney et al, 1997). Second, even women who stay in an occupational pension scheme until retirement receive less due to the gender pay gap and to periods of part-time employment. Third, women's tendency to have a flatter earnings profile with age means they gain less from a final salary pension scheme, in which the amount of pension depends on earnings in the last few years. Women's lower earnings relative to men also reduce their ability to make AVCs to an occupational pension scheme above the compulsory minimum (Price and Ginn, 2003).

Despite the wider access to private pension coverage offered by personal pensions, the gender gap remains substantial. In the mid-1990s, just over half of adults aged 20-59 were contributing to some form of private pension, 64% of men but only 38% of women (Ginn and Arber, 2000a; and see Table 2.1a). A third of adults contributed to an occupational pension scheme and 19% to a personal pension. Among employees, 81% of men but only 56% of women contributed to a private pension. Just over half (52%) belonged to an occupational pension scheme, 61% of men and 42% of women (see Table 2.1b). Only 23% of women part-timers were members. Personal pensions were held by 17% of employees, 20% of men and 14% of women. Thus among employees the gender gap in occupational pensions is replicated in personal pensions, with women's coverage only about 70% of men's. The gender difference among all adults is wider because of women's lower employment participation rates.

Considering only gender differences in private pension coverage masks important variations among women. Later chapters explore variation according to ethnicity (Chapter Three) and partnership and maternal status (Chapters Four and Five). The next section examines class differences in men's and women's private pension coverage.

Table 2.1: Percentage contributing to a private pension, women and men aged 20-59

	a) All adults			b) Employees				
	All	**Men**	**Women**	**All**	**Men**		**Women**	
						FT	**PT**	**All**
Has private pension	*51*	*64*	*38*	*69*	*81*	*72*	*34*	*56*
Employee, occupational pension	32	40	25	52	61	56	23	42
Employee, personal pension	11	13	9	17	20	16	11	14
Self-employed, personal pension	6	9	2					
Not employed, personal pension	2	2	2					
No private pension	*49*	*36*	*62*	*31*	*19*	*28*	*66*	*44*
Employee	19	12	27	31	19	28	66	44
Self-employed	4		6	3				
Not employed	26		18	32				
Column %	100	100	100	100	100	100	100	100
N=	24,069	11,756	12,313	15,056	7,603	7,453	4,260	3,175

Note: FT (full-time) employment is defined here as 31+ hours/week.

Source: Ginn and Arber (2000a), using data from the GHS 1993-94 combined

Class differences in private pensions

Whereas men and those previously in middle-class occupations generally have occupational pensions to cushion them from cuts in state pensions, this is less so for men and women in manual occupations. The class bias of occupational pensions has been well documented (Sinfield, 1978; Hannah, 1986; Arber, 1989; Ginn and Arber, 1991, 1993), and is additional to the effects of earnings, hours of work, sector of employment, and job duration. Among employees aged 20-59, manual workers in 1987 were far less likely to belong to a scheme than non-manual, even after controlling for all these factors as well as age group (Ginn and Arber, 1993). The effect of occupational class was even more marked for women than for men. For example, the odds of membership for a woman in an unskilled manual occupation were only a fifth of the odds for a woman working in a professional occupation or as a manager in a large organisation and only a quarter of the odds for a woman in a routine non-manual occupation.

One important reason for class inequality in occupational pension scheme membership is that certain types of employers, mainly larger organisations, are more likely to offer such a scheme. With the introduction of personal pensions, however, access to a private pension became theoretically available to all employees. Figure 2.1 shows differences in coverage by occupational and personal pensions among employees, according to socioeconomic category (SEC), gender and hours of work.

Figure 2.1: Private pension contributions of employees by gender, socioeconomic category and hours of work of women

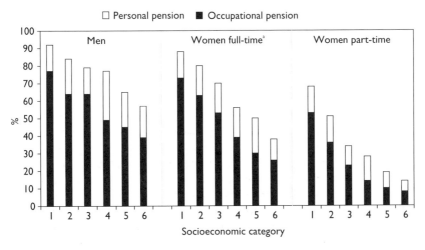

Note: For key to socioeconomic categories, see Table 2.2; [a] 31+ hours per week.

Source: Ginn and Arber (1999), using data from the GHS 1993-94 combined

The small proportion of women employed as professionals and managers in large organisations (SEC 1) retained much of their advantage in private pension coverage even if they worked part time. Part-timers in this occupational group had a pension coverage rate (71%) exceeding that of women employed full time in routine non-manual occupations (SEC 3) or in manual occupations (SECs 4, 5 and 6). However, high occupational status is rare among part-timers. Only 13% of women employed as professionals and managers (SEC 1) worked part time, while half of women in routine non-manual occupations (SEC 3) did so. The class gradient in private pensions coverage was mainly due to occupational pensions, reflecting their differential availability, and the decline in coverage with socioeconomic group was steeper for women than for men.

Personal pension coverage, in contrast, was more evenly distributed among socioeconomic groups, reflecting wider availability of this type of pension. However, personal pensions benefit those in higher socioeconomic groups and full-timers most. For part-timers and the low paid, predominantly women, the advisability of choosing a personal pension (including stakeholder pensions) is doubtful, especially if they cannot be sure of many years of high earnings in the future. Computer simulation of a range of hypothetical employment trajectories of women has illustrated this point (Falkingham and Rake, 2001). These authors estimate that a person retiring in 2050 would need to have earned above women's average wages and have been employed full time for 47 years in order to obtain a combined basic pension and stakeholder pension above the level of means-tested benefits – a tall order. Their calculations for the stakeholder pension were made before the 2001 fall in investment returns and hence should be regarded as optimistic.

In the context of the shift in the public–private mix of pensions, it is important to understand which social groups opted to contribute to the different second tier pension schemes. The remainder of the chapter draws on research (Ginn and Arber, 2000a) focusing on how pension choices have been exercised by employees.

Pension choices made by employees

Personal pensions, introduced in 1988, were intended for employees who might benefit from a private pension, yet were unable to join an occupational pension scheme – either because their employer did not operate a scheme or because they were ineligible under the scheme's rules, as was the often the case for part-timers. Half a million employees were expected to sign up for a personal pension but due to the over-generous financial incentives offered in the late 1980s, five million were contributing to a personal pension by 1993 (DSS, 1994, p 9). Personal pension coverage among employees rose between 1988 and 1994 from 8 to 13% for women and from 15 to 22% for men; by 1995, coverage of working age employees was 28% for full-time men, 22% for full-time women and 11% for part-time women (ONS, 1997). An unexpectedly large number of occupational pension scheme members were persuaded to switch to a personal pension in circumstances likely to provide poorer benefits – the notorious mis-selling of personal pensions, while others opted out of the State Earnings-Related Pension Scheme (SERPS). In order to understand what characteristics were associated with the likelihood of employees rejecting an occupational for a personal pension or choosing a personal pension in preference to SERPS, data from two years of the General Household Survey (GHS) combined, 1993 and 1994, were analysed (Ginn and Arber, 2000a).

Employees' pension options are summarised graphically in Figure 2.2, which shows the proportions of employees taking each pathway. The 63% with access to an occupational pension scheme had three options: to belong to their employer's scheme (52%), to reject it for a personal pension (5%), or reject it and make no private pension contributions (6%). The 37% of employees lacking access had two alternatives: to contribute to a personal pension (12%) or not (25%). The majority of employees with no private pension arrangements must contribute to SERPS, although some, mainly women employed part-time, were paid too little to contribute to National Insurance.

Figure 2.2: Pension arrangements of British employees aged 20-59

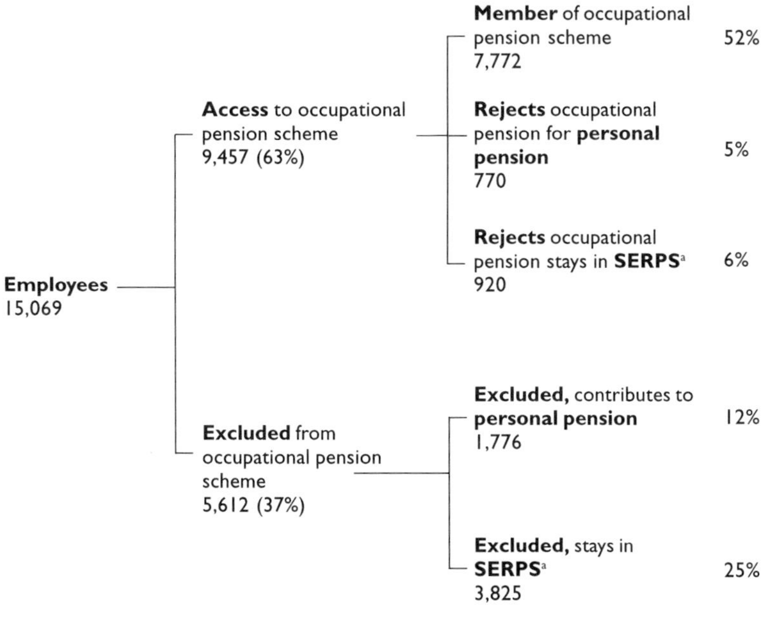

Note: [a] A minority currently paid no SERPS contributions because earnings were too low.
Source: Ginn and Arber (2000a), using data from the GHS for 1993-94 combined

Three main groups of employees can be distinguished:

- **Members**: the 52% who belonged to an occupational pension scheme
- **Rejectors**: the 11% who could belong to an occupational pension scheme but chose not to
- **Excluded**: the 37% who could not join an occupational pension scheme.

The characteristics of these three groups of employees are shown in Table 2.2. As expected, both access to an occupational pension scheme and membership were associated with being male, being aged over 30 (Table 2.2a) and with higher socioeconomic category (SEC) (Table 2.2b).

Among employees with access to an occupational pension scheme, analysis showed that women, especially those working part time, were more likely than men to be rejectors (see Figure 2.3a). For men and for women employed full time, there was a near-linear relationship between age group and proportion of rejectors, while among women part-timers, the proportion of rejectors was high in all age groups at around 40%, only falling below 30% among those in

Table 2.2: Percentage who were Members, Rejectors and Excluded, by age group and socioeconomic category, men and women employees aged 20-59

	Men			Women (full-time)			Women (part-time)		
	Member	Rejector	Excluded	Member	Rejector	Excluded	Member	Rejector	Excluded
All	61	9	30	56	14	30	23	13	64
a) Age group									
20-29	42	14	44	44	19	37	20	12	68
30-39	63	10	27	61	13	26	24	15	61
40-49	71	6	23	63	11	26	22	15	63
50-59	68	5	27	64	7	29	24	10	66
b) Socioeconomic category									
1	78	8	14	73	12	15	55	12	33
2	65	7	28	64	13	23	38	15	47
3	66	11	23	55	14	31	24	12	64
4	51	10	39	40	15	45	15	16	69
5	47	11	42	31	16	53	12	14	74
6	42	11	47	30	25	45	11	13	76

Key to socioeconomic categories: 1 Professionals/managers in large organisations; 2 Intermediate non-manual/managers in small organisations; 3 Routine non-manual; 4 Skilled manual; 5 Semi-skilled manual; 6 Unskilled manual; Excluded: Never worked; Armed forces, full time students, inadequately described.

Source: Ginn and Arber (2000a), using data from the GHS 1993-94 combined

Figure 2.3: Percentage rejecting an occupational pension scheme, among men and women employees with access

a) By age group and hours of work of women

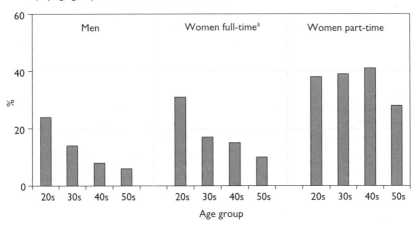

b) By socioeconomic category and hours of work of women

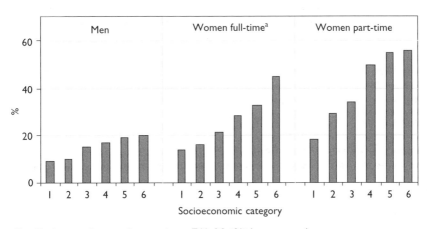

Note: For key to socioeconomic categories see Table 2.2; [a] 31+ hours per week.

Source: Ginn and Arber (2000a), using data from the GHS for 1993-94 combined

their fifties. This high rate of rejection of an occupational pension scheme is likely to reflect part-timers' lower pay irrespective of age group. Some confirmation of this was provided by analysing according to socioeconomic category (see Figure 2.3b). Among women part-timers in the highest level occupations, the proportion of rejectors was relatively low, only slightly higher than for women full-timers in these occupational groups. In addition to younger age and lower socioeconomic category, rejecting an available employer's scheme was found to be associated with lower earnings, shorter job duration and working in a smaller organization (Ginn and Arber, 2000a).

Take-up of personal pensions

This section examines personal pension take-up, distinguishing between rejectors and the excluded. Employees in both these groups would by default remain in SERPS unless their earnings were below the Lower Earning Limit for NI contributions. For brevity, we refer to these low-paid employees as remaining in SERPS.

Among rejectors (11% of employees) men were more likely to have a personal pension (63%) than women full-timers (42%) and part-timers (22%) (see Figure 2.4). For men and women employed full time, those in their thirties were most likely to have a personal pension, while part-timers showed a different pattern, with those aged 30-49 least likely to contribute. Take-up was more common among those in higher socioeconomic groups and with higher earnings (Ginn and Arber, 2000a).

Among the excluded (37% of employees), take-up of a personal pension was more likely for men (48%) than for women full-timers (34%) and part-timers (12%) (see Figure 2.5). Comparing Figures 2.4 and 2.5, the pattern of take-up by rejectors and excluded according to age group is similar, although the proportions of the excluded contributing to a personal pension were lower in each population sub-group than among rejectors, and among women part-timers there was less variation with age group among the excluded.

Multivariate analysis confirmed that personal pensions had found their target among employees lacking access to an occupational pension: take-up among the excluded was highest among the relatively young and well paid (Ginn and Arber, 2000a). However, take-up by those who were less advantaged in the labour market, especially women, is a matter of concern. If individuals were likely to have been better off in SERPS, this constitutes mis-selling.

Figure 2.4: Percentage of Rejectors contributing to a personal pension, by age group and hours of work of women, men and women aged 20-59

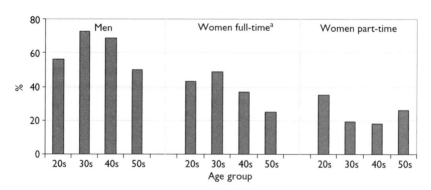

Note: [a] 31+ hours per week.

Source: Ginn and Arber (2000a), using data from the GHS for 1993-94 combined

Figure 2.5: Percentage of Excluded contributing to a personal pension, by age group and hours of work of women, men and women aged 20-59

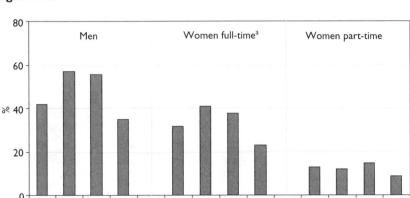

Note:[a] 31+ hours per week.

Source: Ginn and Arber (2000a), using data from the GHS for 1993-94 combined

Mis-selling of personal pensions to rejectors and excluded

A personal pension was expected to provide a better return on contributions than SERPS if, in the long run, the rate of interest exceeded the growth in national earnings. Experts estimated that opting out of SERPS into a personal pension would not be advantageous for those earning below £200 per week (in 1993) (Durham, 1994). Contributing to a personal pension when young and switching back into SERPS between age 30 and 40 has been considered the optimal strategy on average (Dilnot et al, 1994). In the following analysis of personal pension contributors, it is assumed that those who in 1993-94 were earning less than £200 per week or were aged over 40 were probably ill-advised to contract out of SERPS into a personal pension.

In all, half of rejectors were apparently subject to mis-selling and 68% of the excluded (see Figure 2.6, first two bars). The proportions of mis-sold pensions among women were much higher, 62% and 83%, and over 90% among part-timers. Among men who had taken up personal pensions, mis-selling was mainly due to their being aged over 40 but among women it was mainly due to low earnings, especially among part-timers. The extent of personal pension mis-selling to women employed part time (who comprised 14% of all personal pension contributors) is surprising, as is the fact that a quarter of women part-timers with a personal pension reported current earnings below the Lower Earnings Limit. Mis-selling to employees excluded from access to an occupational pensions scheme received far less publicity than mis-selling to

Figure 2.6: Percentage of personal pension contributors over age 40 or paid less than £200 per week, by gender, hours of work and whether Rejector or Excluded from an occupational pension, men and women aged 20-59

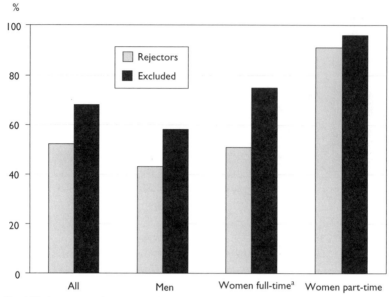

Note: [a] 31+ hours per week.

Source: Ginn and Arber (2000a), using data from the GHS for 1993-94 combined

rejectors, despite the former group being more disadvantaged in the labour market.

To put these findings in the broader context of all employees in the mid-1990s, of the 48% of employees who did not belong to an occupational pension (see Figure 2.2), over a third (or 17% of all employees) contributed to a personal pension. Among these personal pension contributors, 63% were apparently mis-sold a personal pension, according to the criteria used here. As a proportion of all employees, rejectors who were mis-sold represent nearly 3% and the excluded 8%, with women over-represented in both groups. These estimates of mis-selling are inevitably crude, since the outcome will depend on the performance of particular personal pensions as well as on the level and continuity of the individual's future earnings and on macro-economic developments far into the future. However, recent research using longitudinal data from the British Household Panel Survey has shown that low earners are particularly likely to have gaps in pension scheme membership (Banks et al, 2002), reinforcing the adverse effects of low pay on their eventual pension.

The pension choices available since 2001 differ in detail from those in the mid-1990s but similar principles apply. The State Second Pension (S2P) boosts the return on contributions for the low paid through an enhanced accrual rate on low earnings, compared with SERPS, while stakeholder pensions (SHPs) provide a lower cost, easily transferable, form of personal pension (but with a similar risk of poor investment returns). According to a report by the Association of British Insurers (ABI), only about 750,000 SHPs were taken up in the first year since their introduction in 2001, compared with the expected 2.5 million (Griffiths, 2002). The ABI survey found that, despite government hopes that these new pensions would help to narrow the gender difference in private pension coverage, only a third were sold to women. The majority of SHPs were sold to those earning between £10,000 and £30,000 per annum, somewhat higher than the target range of £10,000 to £20,000. The poor take-up is likely to reflect the fact that most of those wishing to contribute to a private pension were already doing so, and also the gloomy projections for investment returns in any type of defined contribution scheme. One commentator observed that if SHP take-up had been a success among the lower paid, "the Government would be heading for the mother of all mis-selling scandals" (Warner, 2002, p 1) since the lower paid would merely deprive themselves of means-tested benefits in retirement – the pensions poverty trap. Whether opting out of the S2P into a SHP is advantageous or not will be hard for either pension providers or individuals to judge as it depends on many unknowns. These include the future structure of rebates for contracting out, the possibility of changes in projected S2P and basic pension amounts and the likely pattern of the individual's future employment and earnings. The Pension Credit, applying from 2003, adds another layer of uncertainty to already difficult decisions for individuals as to whether and when to opt out of the S2P.

Summary and conclusions

The analysis of employees' pension choices in the 1990s indicates that the social groups for whom personal pensions were intended took up the option in large numbers. However, this policy success was marred by extensive mis-selling involving over 10% of all British employees, mainly low-paid women. The implications for women's retirement income are particularly serious, given that the analysis did not take account of future gaps in their employment, which would further reduce the value of a personal pension.

The fact that those with lowest earnings are least likely to save through a private pension is not surprising. Indeed, for those with low lifetime earnings and gaps in employment, paying into state pensions is a sensible strategy, expected to provide the best value. SERPS, and its successor the State Second Pension, are user-friendly schemes, being fully portable, giving automatic membership to all employees earning over the Lower Earnings Limit and providing a defined benefit. However, as noted in Chapter One, the combination of basic and second tier state pensions, even if received in full, is projected to provide an income below poverty level – the level of the Minimum Income Guarantee. Most people with low lifetime earnings, mainly women who have raised a family, can expect a pension income at poverty level whatever choice they make, unless state pensions are substantially improved.

Pension policy since 1986 has been portrayed as improving choice and encouraging individuals to take responsibility for their own retirement income by investing in a private pension. Yet widening second-tier pension choices confront individuals with decisions that even experts find difficult to make. This is especially so for women, whose career earnings and employment participation are more variable and unpredictable than those of men. Those who are most disadvantaged in the labour market tend to have less knowledge of pensions, less access to the most advantageous type of private pension and lower earnings from which to make contributions. Pension policy since the 1980s has led many low-paid employees to spend their contributions on personal pensions unlikely to provide a worthwhile return. Financial incentives to contract out of state pensions have diverted resources from the National Insurance Fund and incurred substantial costs to taxpayers.

The stated aim of policy makers in the 1980s, to reduce poverty in later life by increasing their pension saving through the private sector, seems a vain hope given the failure of private pensions to deliver during a bear market. The crisis of confidence in pensions among working age individuals is understandable: government reforms over two decades have eroded the cash value of state pensions while the inherent fragility of private pension promises has become painfully evident. Unlike the stampede to personal pensions in the 1990s, take-up of stakeholder pensions has been much lower than expected. Some means to insure private pensions, for example through an industry-wide levy to be used in the event of scheme insolvency, could help to restore confidence in private pensions, while top-up payments by government into private pensions on behalf of carers would help make saving more worthwhile for women. However, using public resources to shore up failures in the market would, it has been argued, involve unacceptable moral hazard, subsidising incompetent or corrupt pension providers. Moreover, top-up payments in private pensions would seem an inefficient way to support disadvantaged groups, compared with improving state pensions.

The risk of non-optimal pension choices applies to all, but is especially likely among the low paid, who cannot afford independent advice. Unfortunate decisions are also more serious for those whose pension income is already likely to be low, such as the majority of women and those working in manual occupations. As the next chapter shows, this also applies to ethnic groups who are disadvantaged in the labour market.

THREE

Pension prospects for minority ethnic groups

This chapter examines the pension arrangements made by British men and women of working age from five minority ethnic groups – Indian, black, Chinese/other, Pakistani and Bangladeshi, compared with white. Key questions are the extent to which private pension coverage is lower for men and women from each ethnic minority, compared with white people; whether ethnic differences in coverage relate mainly to variation in employment participation; whether gender inequality in pension coverage is similar across all ethnic groups; and whether the influence of motherhood on employment and pension scheme membership applies equally to women from each ethnic group. The chapter is based on research using three years of the British Family Resources Survey combined, 1994/95, 1995/96 and 1996/97 (Ginn and Arber, 2000b, 2001). First, the income and receipt of private pensions by older men and women from minority ethnic groups are compared with that of white people.

Incomes of older men and women from minority ethnic groups

Incomes of older British individuals from minority ethnic groups are on average lower than those of white people and reliance on means-tested income support is greater (Berthoud, 1998), with particularly high rates of poverty among minority ethnic women who are not married. In each ethnic group older women's personal income is lower than men's (Ginn and Arber, 2000b). In terms of other measures of wealth – car ownership and housing tenure – older people from minority ethnic groups tend to be disadvantaged, although certain ethnic groups such as Indians and Chinese have rates of home ownership comparable with that of white people.

White men aged over 60 had a median personal income of £141 per week in the mid-1990s, compared with only £120 for black people, Indian and Chinese/other men (see Table 3.1, first two columns). Although the Pakistani/ Bangladeshi group of men had a higher income, this must be set against the very low income of women in this group. The gender gap in income was least among black people (Table 3.1, third column). Thus among those aged over 60, white women's median income was 62% of men's but black women's was 80% of black men's. The gender gap in income was wider for older Indians than for white people and wider still for older Pakistanis/Bangladeshis. In

Table 3.1: Income of men and women aged 60+ by ethnicity; women's income as a percentage of men's; and proportion receiving any private pension

	Income[a]		Women's income/men's	% with private pension[b]	
	Men £/wk	Women £/wk	%	Men %	Women %
Black	120	96	80	44	35
White	141	87	62	66	37
Chinese/other	120	74	62	39	31
Indian	120	65	54	38	15
Pakistani/Bangladeshi	150	38	25	15	12

Notes: [a] Median gross personal income. [b] Includes survivors' pensions.

Source: Ginn and Arber (2000b), using data from Family Resources Surveys 1994-96

those ethnic groups where a relatively high proportion of women received a private pension (Table 3.1, fifth column), the gender gap in income was least, despite the often low amounts of such pensions. Apart from men in the Pakistani/ Bangladeshi group, who had a high income despite a low proportion receiving a private pension, income advantage was linked to private pension receipt.

Lack of private pension income among older people from minority ethnic groups is likely to stem from shorter employment records in Britain for the largely migrant older ethnic population, as well as from discriminatory processes in the labour market, limited type and availability of jobs in areas of settlement and sometimes lack of fluency in English. For migrant women, additional barriers may have prevented private pension acquisition, depending on the cultural norms surrounding women's employment, in each specific ethnic group.

In the working age population, as well as the older, the labour market position of minority ethnic groups relative to the majority white population is influenced by the timing and circumstances of migration. Since gender and family circumstances of women influence employment participation and pension arrangements, we can expect to find structural inequalities in employment, earnings and private pension acquisition within each minority ethnic group.

Review of employment and income of ethnic minorities in Britain

Among working-age members of minority ethnic groups an increasing proportion are British-born. However, migration occurred at different times and under different circumstances for each ethnic group. The peak immigration period for Caribbeans was in the early 1960s, while that of Indians and Pakistanis was somewhat later, mainly from 1959 to 1974, and was typically male-led, with younger wives following (Cooper et al, 1999). It was not until the 1980s that immigration from Bangladesh and Hong Kong occurred in significant numbers (Modood and Berthoud, 1997). Because of diverse migration circumstances and the varying extent to which each group has suffered racism and discrimination, it is not surprising that the different ethnic groups vary in employment rates, earnings, household income, educational qualifications and English fluency, as well as in age structure and average time of residence in Britain.

Pakistani and Bangladeshi households are characterised by high male unemployment and low economic activity of women, low pay and large families. Afro-Caribbean men have an unemployment rate twice that of white men at 31% (Modood and Berthoud, 1997) and those who are employed earn low average wages (Berthoud, 1998). Male self-employment is high, as a proportion of the economically active, among Chinese (28%) and Indians (25%), compared with Pakistanis (21%) and white men (18%); but among male Afro-Caribbeans it is only 9% (Modood and Berthoud, 1997).

Employment rates of women vary markedly by ethnicity (Owen, 1994), reflecting the gender ideologies and traditions characteristic of each ethnic group, as well as the race discrimination experienced by both men and women. Britain has a high part-time employment rate among married mothers, concentrated in lower level occupations or grades (McRae, 1993; Macran et al, 1996) but the effect of marriage and of having young children at home on women's employment participation and hours of work differs among ethnic groups. For example, married Pakistani and Bangladeshi women have very low rates of economic activity, even where there are no dependent children, while for white women the presence of dependent children is associated with reduced economic activity and part-time work (Dale and Holdsworth, 1998). Among employed women with children, minority ethnic women are more likely than white women to work full time, irrespective of their occupational group (Holdsworth and Dale, 1997; Dale and Holdsworth, 1998).

The ability to contribute to a private pension scheme depends on employment and the availability of surplus income after immediate needs of the household have been met. Recent research has confirmed the higher household poverty rate of ethnic minorities compared with white people, but the incidence of poverty varies considerably among ethnic groups (Berthoud, 1998). For example, half of Pakistani and Bangladeshi households with at least one member in employment have an income below half average household income (net equivalent income before housing costs). This compares with 18% of Chinese, 15% of Indian, 8% of Caribbean, 9% of African, and 9% of white.

Black and other ethnic minority individuals earn less on average than white people, but the gender gap varies within each ethnic group While British women full timers earned 82% of men's hourly rate in 2000 (ONS, 2001), among black Africans and Caribbeans, the proportion (in 1996) was higher at 87% of men's, and among Indians it was 88% (Modood and Berthoud, 1997). These ethnic and gender differences in earnings can be expected to influence patterns of private pension scheme contributions and hence income in later life.

Previous research on private pension coverage according to ethnicity focused on employees. For example, Peggs (1995), using the General Household Survey, found that among male employees, membership of occupational pension schemes in 1988-90 ranged from 62% (white) to 47% (Indian). Among women employees, Afro-Caribbeans had the highest occupational pension coverage at 55% compared with Pakistani/Bangladeshi (43%), Indian (38%) and white (37%). In interpreting these figures, it must be remembered that in certain ethnic groups women's employment rates are very low. In the five years following the introduction of personal pensions for employees in 1988, coverage by these pensions expanded rapidly. Research by Burton (1997) on employed individuals aged 18 to 65 in 1992-93 showed that while occupational and personal pension coverage among employed white men was 76%, it remained much lower for employed men in minority ethnic groups. Among employed women, however, private pension coverage was not highest among whites. Coverage was estimated as 57% (black), 51% (white and Indian), 45% (other) and zero (Pakistani/ Bangladeshi).

To obtain a more complete picture of the pension prospects of all men and women from minority ethnic groups (whether employed or not) and to compare with the white majority, employment and private pension scheme coverage was analysed for the whole working age population, using the Family Resources Survey (FRS) (Ginn and Arber, 2001). The FRS is a large-scale, annual, nationally representative survey of individuals living in private households, carried out by the Department of Social Security (DSS, 1996). By combining the FRS for 1994/95 1995/96 and 1996/97, a sample of over 97,000 adults aged 20-59 (including over 5,700 from ethnic minorities) was obtained. In the survey, ethnicity was self-defined. Respondents were shown a list and asked, "To which of these groups do you consider yourself to belong? White (UK or other), Black African, Black Caribbean, Black other, Indian, Pakistani, Bangladeshi, Chinese and Other." In most of the analysis, these were grouped into six categories – white, Indian, black (including black African, black Caribbean and black other), Chinese/other, Pakistani and Bangladeshi. In order to compare how motherhood affects private pension coverage in each ethnic group, women's pension coverage was analysed according to their lifecourse stage. Women were grouped according to lifecourse stage:

1. Aged under 35 with no dependent child;
2. Youngest child aged under 10;
3. Youngest child aged 10 or over;
4. Women aged 35 and over with no dependent child.

For analysis by lifecourse stage, Pakistani and Bangladeshi women were combined in one group and Chinese and other groups were excluded, due to their small numbers in some lifecourse stages.

Employment of working-age men and women in the six ethnic groups

Full-time employees are relatively advantaged in private pension acquisition, in that they are more likely to have access to occupational pension schemes and also can make higher contributions. Figure 3.1 shows the proportions of men and women employed full time in each ethnic group, by 10-year age group.

Figure 3.1: Percentage employed full time by ethnicity and age group, men and women aged 20-59

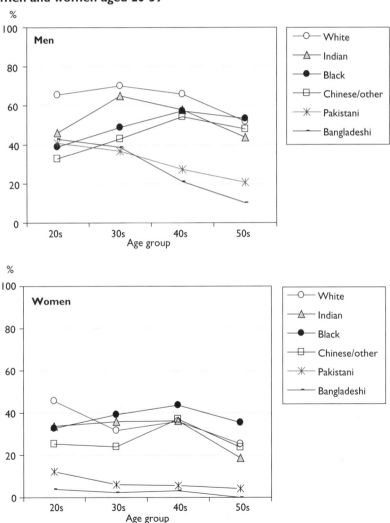

Source: Ginn and Arber (2001), using data from Family Resources Surveys 1994-96

The proportions employed full time, part time and self-employed are shown in Appendix Table A3.1. Compared with white men, men in all other ethnic groups had lower rates of full-time employment and this was particularly marked among Pakistani and Bangladeshi men aged over 40. The peak age group for full-time employment was in their thirties for white and Indian men, their forties for black and Chinese/other men and in their twenties for Pakistani and Bangladeshi men. The rate of self-employment increased with age group but was low at all ages for black men. Part-time employment was rare among men, although higher among Bangladeshis than other ethnic groups (Table A3.1).

As expected, the proportion of women employed full time was lower than for men in each ethnic group, although the gender difference was small for black people. The peak age group for women's full-time employment varied with ethnicity. Whereas the peak age for white women's full-time employment was in their twenties, it was in their forties for black, Chinese/other and Indian women. Very low proportions of Pakistani and Bangladeshi women were employed full time, under 15% (Figure 3.1). Part-time employment, although high among white women aged over 30, was relatively low among women in the minority ethnic groups (Table A3.1). Among Indian, black and Chinese/other women who were employed, most were full-time employees. A low proportion of Pakistani women was employed, under 20% among those aged over 30, and self-employment accounted for about half of all employment in this group. Bangladeshi women had the lowest employment rate, less than 10%, with the majority of these working part time or self-employed.

The amount of both state and private pension entitlements that can be accumulated is reduced for those with few years employed in Britain because of migration in mid life. For second tier pensions, the amount depends not only on the duration of employment but also on the proportion of employment that was full time, since part-time earnings are generally low. Figure 3.2 shows, for men and women in each ethnic group, the proportion of years for which they had been employed full time in Britain (as an employee or self-employed) since the age of 16, based on self report. Among men, white men had been employed full time for over 80% of the time, compared with 65% for Indians, 58% for Bangladeshis, 55% for black men and Pakistanis and 50% for Chinese/other. White women had been employed full time for just under half the time, followed by black (43%), Chinese/other and Indian (each 36%), Pakistani (11%) and Bangladeshi women (6%). Thus white men and women had longer full-time employment than their counterparts in other ethnic groups, indicating advantage in second tier pension prospects. Among women, the difference between white people and black people was small. The very short duration of full-time employment of Pakistani and Bangladeshi women, relative to all other women, was striking and indicated that they could expect very little pension income of their own in retirement. Gender differences outweighed those associated with ethnicity, especially for Pakistanis and Bangladeshis. These results should be treated with some caution, due to the unreliability of recall data.

Figure 3.2: Percentage of years employed full time since age 16 by ethnicity, men and women aged 20-59

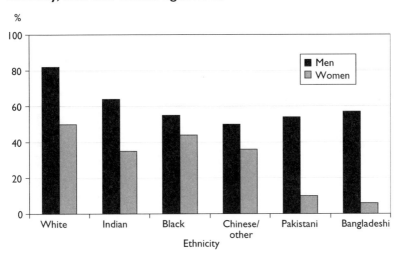

Source: Ginn and Arber (2001), using data from Family Resources Survey 1994-96

The next section analyses the private pension arrangements of men and women in the six ethnic groups.

Private pension coverage

The proportion of working age men and women in each ethnic group who were contributing to three types of private pension – occupational, personal and pensions for the self-employed – is shown in Table 3.2. Among men, white men were most likely to contribute to a private pension scheme of any kind (61%), followed by Indians (46%), black men (35%), Chinese/other (33%), Pakistanis (17%) and only 9% of Bangladeshi men. White women were also the most likely to contribute to a private pension but a slightly different ethnic hierarchy of pension coverage was evident for women: white (37%), black (30%), Indian (26%), Chinese/other (23%), Pakistani (6%) and Bangladeshi (3%). The near gender equality in private pension coverage among black people may reflect both the pension advantage of black women employed in the public sector, especially the National Health Service (NHS), and the disadvantage of black men, among whom unemployment is high. The gender difference in private pension coverage was substantial in every other ethnic group.

Within each ethnic-gender group, occupational pensions were far more common than personal pensions but the balance between the types of pension scheme varied. Pensions for the self-employed were most likely among white, Indian and Chinese/other men (Table 3.2). Despite a high rate of self-employment among Pakistani and Bangladeshi men, only a small proportion

Table 3.2: Private pension arrangements of men and women aged 20-59 by ethnicity (column percentages)

Men	White	Indian	Black	Chinese/ other	Pakistani	Bangladeshi
Occupational pension[a]	39	31	26	21	13	5
Personal pension only	13	8	8	6	2	1
Self-employed pension	9	7	2	6	2	2
No private pension, employed	19	28	24	27	38	43
Not employed	20	26	41	40	45	48
N=	43,701	725	683	625	429	139

Women	White	Indian	Black	Chinese/ other	Pakistani	Bangladeshi
Occupational pension[a]	27	19	24	17	6	3
Personal pension only	8	5	5	4	0	0
Self-employed pension	2	2	1	2	0	0
No private pension, employed	29	31	23	24	14	7
Not employed	34	43	47	53	80	90
N=	47,050	809	947	734	466	171

Notes: [a] Some of those with an occupational pension also contributed to a personal pension. Columns do not all add to exactly 100% due to rounding.

Source: Ginn and Arber (2001), using data from Family Resources Surveys 1994-96

contributed to a pension for the self-employed. Among men who had private pension coverage, three quarters of black and Pakistani men belonged to an occupational pension scheme, compared with about two thirds for the other ethnic groups. Among women with coverage, nearly three quarters belonged to an occupational pension scheme. Personal pensions were particularly rare among Pakistani and Bangladeshi women.

The proportion in each ethnic-gender group who can contribute to a private pension is limited by the extent to which they are in paid employment. However, among employed Pakistanis and Bangladeshis the proportions lacking pension coverage was very high, over 70% (Table 3.2). This suggests considerable scope for increased coverage; we return later to the question of why a high proportion of employed individuals might lack private pension coverage.

Occupational pension contributions in the midlife years, when earnings are often highest, have a disproportionate influence on later life income, and indicate the likely pattern of private pension income for the next generation of pensioners. Figure 3.3 shows private pension coverage (including both occupational and personal pensions) among men and women in their forties and fifties. The pension disadvantage of Pakistanis and Bangladeshis, severe in their forties, is

Figure 3.3: Percentage with private pension cover by ethnicity and age group, men and women aged 40-59

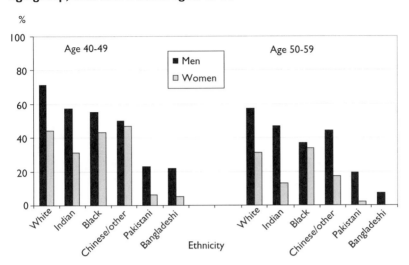

Source: Ginn and Arber (2001), using data from the Family Resources Surveys 1994-96

even more pronounced for Bangladeshis in their fifties. The lower rates of coverage among both men and women in their fifties reflect falling employment rates with advancing age. Women's private pension disadvantage compared with men was evident in each ethnic group, except for black people in their fifties, where coverage rates were almost equal.

Women's lifecourse stage, employment and pension coverage

Women's participation in employment, and hence their ability to contribute to a private pension, is related to their lifecourse stage, a concept combining age and maternal status. Women from each ethnic group were most likely to be employed full time in the first stage (aged under 35, childless) and least likely in the second (youngest child aged under 10). However, the clear association between the full-time employment rate and age of youngest child found among white women did not apply equally to the other ethnic groups. For example, among Indian and black women, full-time employment was more common for those whose youngest child was aged over 10 than for those aged over 35 with no dependent child at home.

Private pension coverage of women in each lifecourse stage broadly reflected the proportions employed full time, although for black women their pension coverage was low relative to their high rates of full-time employment. Very low proportions of Pakistani and Bangladeshi women contributed to a private pension, under 10% in any lifecourse stage (Figure 3.4). Among young childless women, less than a third of women in the ethnic minority groups had pension

Figure 3.4: Percentage with private pension cover by ethnicity and lifecourse stage, women aged 20-59

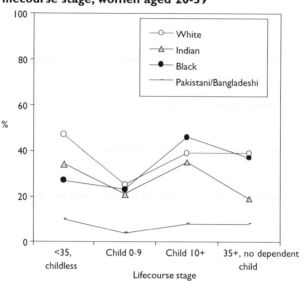

Source: Ginn and Arber (2001), using data from the Family Resources Surveys 1994-96

coverage, compared with nearly half of white women. Among those with a young child, barely a fifth of white, Indian and black women had pension coverage. Coverage rates rose among women with a child aged over 10, especially for black women, where 46% were covered. For black and Indian women aged over 35 with no dependent child, pension coverage rates fell to a lower level, reflecting their lower full-time employment rates in this lifecourse stage. White women, in contrast, had similar rates of pension coverage in the latter two lifecourse stages (40%).

Multivariate analysis

Occupational class influences access to a good occupational pension scheme (see Chapter Two). Therefore the concentration of ethnic minorities in more disadvantaged segments of the labour market (Modood and Berthoud, 1997) reduces their pension prospects, in addition to shorter duration of full-time employment and low earnings relative to household needs. In order to assess how far ethnic differences in private (occupational and personal) pension coverage are explained by variation in family and employment variables, logistic regression analysis was used, successively adding more control variables in a series of five models (Ginn and Arber, 2001 and Appendix Tables A3.2 and A3.3). Figure 3.5 shows, for men and women separately, the odds of private pension coverage, relative to the reference category (white people), whose odds of private pension coverage are defined as 1.00. Odds ratios for only the base

Figure 3.5: Odds ratio of contributing to a private pension by ethnicity, men and women aged 20-59

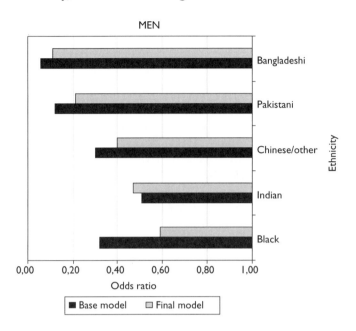

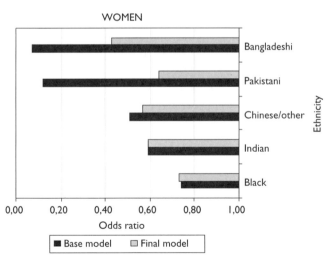

Notes: Figure 3.5 is derived from Appendix Tables A3.2 and A3.3, in which full logistic regression results are shown. All odds ratios are significantly different ($p < 0.01$) from 'whites' as a reference category (defined as 1.00), except for Pakistani and Bangladeshi women in the final model. Variables included in the base model are: five-year age group and ethnicity. Variables included in the final model are: five-year age group, ethnicity, marital and parental status, age finished full-time education, employment status, years employed full time, socioeconomic group, and gross income.

Source: Ginn and Arber (2001), using data from the Family Resources Surveys 1994-96

and final models are shown. The base model includes variables for ethnicity and age group. The final model includes variables controlling for marital and parental status, age of finishing full-time education, employment status and years of full-time employment, socioeconomic category and gross individual income.

The private pension disadvantage of minority ethnic groups compared with white was greater for men than for women, especially for black men. Thus black men had odds of pension coverage in the base model that were only 0.32, compared with 1.00 for white men, after controlling for age group (see Figure 3.5, base model for men). Including variables for marital and parental status showed that married men were far more likely to have private pension cover than non-married (see Table A3.2). Including terminal age of education substantially reduced the odds ratios for black and Chinese/other men, indicating that after taking account of their investment in education these groups suffered a greater pension disadvantage relative to white men than was seen in the base model. The inclusion of employment variables increased the odds ratios of pension coverage for each minority ethnic group, especially for black men. Occupational class and income further raised the odds ratios for each minority ethnic group, somewhat reducing the difference from white men (Table A3.2, final model for men). Nevertheless, after controlling for these family and employment variables, men in minority ethnic groups were still considerably less likely than white men to have private pension cover.

Women in each minority ethnic group also had lower odds of private pension coverage than white women but the difference was relatively small for black women. These women had odds of 0.74, compared with 1.00 for white women after controlling for age group, while the odds ratio for Indian women was 0.59, for Chinese/other 0.51, for Pakistani 0.12 and for Bangladeshi 0.07 (see Figure 3.5, base model for women). Adding variables for marital and parental status raised the odds ratio of pension coverage for black women to 0.85, showing that differences in marital and parental status explain a substantial part of black women's lower private pension coverage compared with white women (see Table A3.3). For the other minority ethnic women the odds ratios were largely unaltered by including marital and parental status in the model. Thus in spite of the important influence these variables had on the chance of pension coverage, the effect was similar for women in each of these four ethnic groups and did not explain their lower pension coverage compared with white women's. Length of full-time education had a substantial effect; women who finished their education at age 17 or 18 had odds of private pension coverage over three times higher than those of women who finished under age 16. Including this variable reduced the odds ratios for black, Indian and Chinese/other women, indicating that the private pension disadvantage of women in these ethnic groups was not explained by lack of education; on the contrary, an even more severe pension disadvantage was revealed. Including employment variables in the model had a marked effect on the odds ratios of pension coverage for Pakistani and Bangladeshi women, increasing them to 0.61 and 0.37 respectively.

Thus low rates of full-time employment explain much of Pakistani and Bangladeshi women's pension coverage deficit compared with white women. Controlling for socioeconomic category and individual income further improved the odds ratio of pension coverage for Chinese/other, Pakistani and Bangladeshi women (see Figure 3.5, final model for women), reflecting these groups' disadvantage, relative to white women, in the occupational distribution.

Comparing the final models for men and women shows that the ethnic differential in pension coverage that remained in the final model, after controlling for relevant employment and other variables, was more severe for men than for women. Whereas lack of participation in paid employment explained most of Pakistani and Bangladeshi women's private pension disadvantage, this was not so for men in these groups (Figure 3.5 and Table A3.2 and A3.3).

The explanation for the residual ethnic differential in private pension coverage may lie partly in minority ethnic men and women having less access to occupational pensions because they are employed in different kinds of organisations than their white counterparts. In small firms in the private sector employers are less likely to operate an occupational pension scheme (Ginn and Arber, 1993; Burton, 1997); employment in such companies may be more common among ethnic minority groups. Among Asian men, relatively high rates of self-employment limited the proportion who could join an occupational pension scheme. For employees lacking access to an occupational pension scheme, the options were to contribute to a personal pension or remain in the State Earnings Related Pension Scheme (SERPS). There are sound reasons why employees may decide against a personal pension (as discussed in Chapter Two) and these may apply disproportionately to those in minority ethnic groups. For the self-employed, who are excluded from SERPS, similar considerations apply. Cultural values among Pakistanis and Bangladeshis are likely to emphasise traditional patterns of inter-generational support, rather than formal pension rights, as found by Nesbitt and Neary (2001) in their research in Oldham. Another possible factor is that minority ethnic groups may experience financial exclusion, in terms of having less information about the British pension system and receiving less attention from those marketing financial products. Among Pakistanis and Bangladeshis, Islamic beliefs concerning receiving interest on investments may also affect willingness to take out a personal pension plan. Further reasons which have been suggested for low personal pension coverage among ethnic minorities are that they lack trust in financial institutions or that personal pension providers have been less assiduous in marketing their products to ethnic minorities.

Conclusions

Among older people, a hierarchy of ethnic groups in terms of median income was evident, with white people most advantaged, followed by black people, then Chinese/other, Pakistani/Bangladeshi and Indian. However, among older women, greater income inequality according to ethnicity was evident than for older men, reflecting the wider gender gap among Pakistanis, Bangladeshis and Indians compared with a smaller gap for black and white people. The gender gap in income was smaller in those ethnic groups where a relatively high proportion of older women received a private pension. Although older men in the Pakistani/Bangladeshi group had a relatively high income on average, this was less due to private pensions than to income from other sources such as means-tested benefits.

Analysis of the employment and private pension coverage of working age individuals has indicated that this pattern is likely to be broadly maintained. Gender and ethnicity interact, creating an ethnic-gender hierarchy of private pension coverage as follows: white men; Indian men; white women; black men; Chinese/other men; black women; Indian women; Chinese/other women; Pakistani men; Bangladeshi men; Pakistani women; Bangladeshi women. Thus white men and women were relatively advantaged and Pakistani and Bangladeshi men and women very disadvantaged in pensions. Gender inequality in private pension coverage was much less among black people than other ethnic groups, mainly because of the low coverage among black men. Marital and parental status influenced the private pension coverage of women, with similar effects for all ethnic groups except black women.

For both men and women, the major factors explaining lower private pension coverage among minority ethnic groups were related to participation in full-time employment, employee status, occupational class and earnings. Family variables only contributed to explaining low coverage for black women and for Chinese/other men. Length of full-time education, far from explaining low pension coverage among minority ethnic groups, appears to be of less importance in predicting private pension contributions for certain ethnic-gender groups compared with white.

A residual minority ethnic disadvantage in private pension coverage, which was more marked for men than for women, was still evident after taking account of differences in the employment factors analysed (employment status, length of full-time employment, occupational class and income). This chapter suggests that among those currently of working age, members of minority ethnic groups, especially women, will be disproportionately dependent on family members or means-tested benefits in later life, due to the combination of low private pension coverage and the policy of shifting pension provision towards the private sector.

FOUR

Changing patterns of partnership: divorce and pensions

Since the 1960s, a more permissive social and legal climate concerning sexual relationships and family forms has led to parallel demographic trends in many western countries. These include rising cohabitation, postponement of marriage, increased divorce rates and extramarital births, increased use of family planning and low fertility rates – a set of changes that has been termed the second demographic transition.

The far-reaching changes in partnership status and parenting create new challenges for a pension system originally based on the male breadwinner–female homemaker model. Public pensions established means of providing pensions for married women and widows (Daly, 1996; Sainsbury, 1996; see also Chapter One), while occupational pensions have also generally provided widows' pensions. At a time when the link between marriage and motherhood was close, such derived rights based on a husband's contribution record ensured that most mothers received some pension compensation for their unpaid childrearing role, as well as for providing domestic services to their family more generally. Yet the separation of the roles of wife and mother, as the link between marriage and childrearing loosens, raises questions for pension schemes – both state and private.

Changing family forms and gender roles are often neglected in analysis of pension policy, where the predominant focus has been state and market, as noted by O'Connor et al (1999).

In this chapter, I first consider issues of equity arising from the growing mismatch between family forms and the acquisition of pension rights through marriage, then review the divergence of marriage and motherhood and the gap in childcare provision in Britain. The chapter then considers how partnership status affects employment and pension acquisition, drawing on research using data from three years of the British General Household Survey (Ginn and Price, 2002) and focusing on the pension prospects of divorced and separated women.

Derived pensions: issues of equity

The generation of women born before 1940 grew up with a pension system based on the male breadwinner–female homemaker model, as outlined in Chapter One. The Beveridge structure of National Insurance discouraged married women from building independent state and private pension entitlements through employment and pension contributions, thus rewarding and reinforcing the male breadwinner model (Allatt, 1981; Baldwin and Falkingham, 1994). Single (never married) women without children were better able than married women to build good pension entitlements from the state and the private sector, as can be seen from their higher average income in retirement (see Chapter One, Table 1.1). However, women who deviated from these two acceptable patterns by bearing a child outside marriage were left to suffer the consequences – generally a poor NI record and low pension income.

Despite major social changes affecting women's lifecourse since the 1940s, derived rights are still common in British state and private pensions (summarised in Table 4.1). At age 60, married women are entitled to a basic NI pension at 60% of their husband's amount provided he is aged at least 65 and receiving the pension. This derived pension may be claimed if it exceeds their own entitlement to the basic pension. From April 2010, the right to a 60% spousal benefit will be extended to husbands, although this derived pension will only rarely exceed the husband's own basic pension entitlement. Widow/ers are entitled to 100% of their deceased spouse's basic pension and until 2002 could also receive up to 100% of their State Pension Scheme (SERPS). For those widowed after October 2002, the SERPS derived pension is limited to a maximum of 50% of the deceased spouse's entitlement.

Divorced women may use their ex-husband's basic pension contribution record for the period of the marriage to boost their own entitlement, although this derived right is lost if they remarry before state pension age. However, at divorce women lose the possibility of a widow's benefit from their husband's state second pension. Women who are legally separated but not divorced retain the legal status of wife and lose no rights in state pension schemes. This is also the case in some occupational pension schemes, although the rules vary.

Occupational final salary pension schemes usually provide derived benefits for widows, widowers and dependants of scheme members, although provisions vary according to the scheme rules and whether the scheme member dies in service or after retirement. Differential treatment of widows and widowers in occupational pension schemes was confirmed as unlawful sex discrimination by the European Court 'Barber' judgment (*Barber v GRE Assurance*, 1990) and the requirement of equal treatment was legislated in the British 1995 Pensions Act. Survivors' pensions in occupational schemes are a fraction (typically half) of the deceased member's entitlement. Divorced women have generally received none of their ex-husband's second tier pension (occupational, personal or SERPS), although legislation operative from 2000 may modify this to some extent (Ginn and Price, 2002). The consequences of divorce for private pensions are considered in detail later in this chapter.

In personal pensions or defined contribution occupational pension schemes, married individuals must, when they convert their fund to an annuity, buy a joint life annuity with that portion of the fund that replaces the state second pension – the 'protected rights' element. The amount of pension is lower than

Table 4.1: Derived entitlements in state and private pension schemes (2002)

	Wives	**Husbands**	**Widows**	**Widowers**	**Divorced**
Basic pension	**60% of husband's pension** if both are over state pension age		**100% of deceased spouse's pension**		**Spouse's NIC record may be used** to improve pension up to a maximum for a single person
SERPS/ State Second Pension	–	–	**50% of spouse's pension** (was 100% until Oct 2002) in addition to own up to maximum for a single person		
Occupational pensions[a]	–	–	**Surviving spouse gets pension** on death in service Discretionary lump sum to surviving spouse or cohabitee **Surviving spouse gets pension** on death in retirement Discretionary pension to surviving cohabitee (in 75% of private sector and 20% of public sector schemes) Discretionary lump sum to surviving spouse or cohabitee (in most private sector and half public sector schemes)		**Divorce court must consider all second-tier pensions** and may order sharing
Personal pensions[b]	–	–	Fund is paid to trustee on death in service, paid to surviving spouse at discretion of trustee **Surviving spouse gets annuity** on death in retirement, based on protected rights[c] portion of the fund		

Notes: **Bold** indicates statutory rights. [a] In occupational pensions, provisions other than for protected rights depend on scheme rules; the most common provisions are shown. [b] Includes stakeholder pensions. [c] In private pensions that are contracted out, only protected rights (the portion of the pension that replaces SERPS/State Second Pension) are statutory.

a single life annuity but ensures that the survivor receives a pension to replace that which they would have received from the state second tier pension. However, for any additional amount above the protected rights element, a single life annuity may be purchased. Wives may not be aware that their survivor's pension will not necessarily be based on the whole of their deceased husband's annuity.

Cohabitees, whether heterosexual, gay or lesbian, have at the time of writing no derived rights to pensions, state or private. In many occupational pension schemes, trustees may exercise discretion in favour of the surviving cohabitee if they are deemed to have been financially dependent on the scheme member. Nevertheless, cohabitees are denied the legal protections allowed to married, widowed and divorced women. Unlike heterosexual couples, same-sex couples (as at 2002) lack the option of marriage or any other way of establishing entitlement to spousal or survivor pensions. Many commentators consider that a European directive coming into force in December 2003 will make such distinctions in pension rights according to marital status unlawful. In 2002 there was cross-party support in Britain for future legislation allowing heterosexual or same-sex couples to register their partnership so as to gain the rights enjoyed by married couples in the areas of pensions, as well as inheritance, tenancy and immigration. The right to register a partnership may be a mixed blessing in financial terms. Claims by registered partners for means-tested benefits in retirement (or earlier) are likely to be subject to a joint means test, as for married couples, and the partners may receive less financial support as a result. Given that means-testing is expected to apply to over half of pensioners from 2003 (see Chapter Seven), couples considering registering their partnership, when this is an option, will need to balance the advantage of obtaining derived pensions against the possible disadvantage of having their income and assets tested jointly.

Equity issues arise because derived pensions involve substantial cross-subsidies from other contributors to pension schemes, as pointed out by Cuvillier (1979) and developed further by Jepsen and Meulders (2002) in the context of social protection in EU countries. Derived pension rights apply irrespective of whether the beneficiary's employment opportunities have been constrained by raising children or caring for other family members. For example, in Britain childless married, widowed and divorced women who have never been in paid employment receive derived pensions through National Insurance. These pensions are funded by the contributions of others, including single and cohabiting mothers who have managed to combine employment with caring for their children. Thus non-married mothers – a financially-disadvantaged group – are subsidising the derived pensions of childless married women. Similarly, in occupational pension schemes there are cross-subsidies from members who are not married – including lone parents – to members who are married; the latter pay no additional contribution into the scheme in respect of the survivor benefits. In personal pensions and defined contribution occupational pensions, in contrast, the cost of a survivor's pension in the form of a joint life annuity is not subsidised by the non-married, since the contributor 'pays' by receiving a lower pension.

It is questionable whether the subsidies to marriage in state pensions and in final salary pension schemes are justifiable in the twenty-first century, given the increasing employment of married women and the rise in lone parenthood. It may be simpler and fairer to phase out derived benefits and replace them with improved pension protection for those with caring commitments. Two factors particularly relevant to this issue – the unravelling tie between marriage and motherhood and the lack of childcare services to help lone mothers maintain employment – are discussed in turn.

Marriage and motherhood: a loosening link

The expectation that women will bear children has declined throughout developed societies. In Britain, a quarter of British women born in 1972 are predicted to be still childless by age 45, compared with only 11% of women born in 1943 (FPSC, 2000). Equally, the expectation that women who do raise children will be married has declined. Among women aged 16-59 with dependent children, only two thirds were married in 2001 (ONS, 2002c), while motherhood outside marriage has risen due to divorce, cohabitation and unpartnered pregnancy. Births outside marriage rose from 7% in the early 1970s to 38% in 1998, with over 60% of these births registered by cohabiting couples (ONS, 1999).

The proportion of British women aged 18-49 who were married fell from three quarters in 1979 to only half in 2001, while those who were single (never married) doubled from 18% to over a third and those who were divorced and separated nearly doubled from 7 to 13% (ONS, 2002c). Among non-married women aged 18-49, the proportion who were cohabiting shot up from 3 to 13% over the same period. In the peak age range for childbearing (25-34), the proportion of women who were cohabiting had reached 22% by 2001 (ONS, 2002c). Although cohabiting mothers potentially benefit from a partner's shared income and help with childcare, cohabiting partnerships are more likely to dissolve than marriage, even after taking account of the presence of children (Buck and Ermisch, 1995). Moreover, cohabiting couples are more likely than married to have a low income, limiting the ability of cohabiting mothers to make pension contributions. As discussed above, cohabiting women lack the legal protections in state and private pensions accorded to married women.

The number of lone parents in Britain rose from 474,000 in 1961 to 1.7 million by 1999 (Haskey, 1994, 1998). Over 90% of lone parents are mothers. Of these, nearly 60% are divorced or separated, while the majority of single mothers are separated from the father of their child after a cohabiting relationship (NCOPF, 2001). Lone parent families represent a quarter of all families (ONS, 2000a). Since only a minority of divorced or separated mothers receive any maintenance from their ex-husband (Marsh et al, 2001), the majority face a financial struggle to raise children single-handed. Over half of lone parents had a gross income of less than £200 per week, compared with a quarter of cohabiting couples and only 13% of married couples (ONS, 2002c). Lone parents' earnings are limited, due to the difficulties of managing childcare and employment (discussed below). This reduces their ability to contribute to pension schemes.

The rise in divorce, lone parenthood and cohabitation is unlikely to be reversed, and the decline of marriage as a lifelong contract makes reliance on a husband for income in later life an increasingly risky strategy for women. Employment has become more necessary for women, not only to meet current household needs but also as the source of independent pension entitlements. Although women's employment has increased (see Chapter One), mothers' employment rates and earnings remain substantially less than for childless women (Ginn and Arber, 2002). Harkness and Waldfogel (1999) show that in the mid-1990s, among men and women aged 24 to 44, the gender gap in employment was 17%. However, the family gap (between childless women and those with children) was much larger at 29% (see Figure 4.1). Among all those who were employed, the gender gap in hourly earnings was 18% for childless women but 30% for those with children – a family gap of about 12%. Those women with children who were employed full time had only a small family gap in hourly earnings, 5% (see Figure 4.2). However, combining motherhood with full-time employment depends on obtaining suitable childcare.

Figure 4.1: Employment by gender and presence of children, men and women aged 24-44

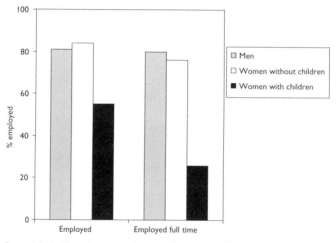

Source: Adapted from Harkness and Waldfogel (1999, Table 1)

Figure 4.2: Hourly earnings of women relative to men by presence of children, men and women aged 24-44

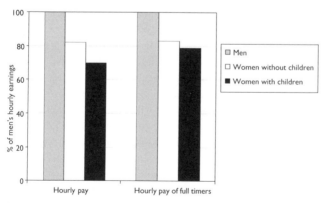

Source: Adapted from Harkness and Waldfogel (1999, Table 2)

The childcare gap and costs

Major obstacles to British mothers' employment are the lack of suitable childcare services and the high fees charged. In 1998 there was only one registered childcare place for every 7.5 children aged under eight in England, including places with childminders, day nurseries and after school clubs (Daycare Trust, 1999). Demand for childcare outstrips supply, creating a "bottleneck that forces mothers of young children to provide parental care rather than possibly participate in the labour force" (Chevalier and Viitanen, 2002, p 22). Despite some increase in the number of registered childminders and nursery places as a result of the Labour government's National Childcare Strategy, there is still a large childcare gap, with day nursery provision especially scarce in poorer areas, where parents cannot afford the fees required to make commercial nurseries financially viable (Daycare Trust, 2000). Childcare services are often unavailable for those who have to adopt 'new work patterns' outside the traditional 9-5, Monday to Friday week. Over 60% of working families have a parent who is employed outside regular 9-5 hours, including early morning, evening, night and weekend shifts (Daycare Trust, 2000). Although such unsocial hours are determined by the employer's needs, the pay premium for weekend work is being eroded, while women evening and night workers, unlike equivalent men, receive no pay premium (Harkness, 2002). Indeed, they earn less than day workers. Undersupply of formal childcare reflects the poor pay and low status of the childcare workforce. But without government support for childcare services the necessary improvements in wages will increase the already high fees charged to parents.

According to a survey in 2002, the typical cost of a nursery place for a child aged under two was £120 per week, with a childminder slightly less expensive at £113 per week (Daycare Trust, 2002). For children aged over two, either a day nursery or a childminder cost an average £112 per week. Where jobs are most plentiful, as in London and the south east, the costs were higher. A live-in nanny (in the late 1990s) cost as much as £260 per week (FPSC, 1998). For low-paid parents employed at least 16 hours per week, help towards the cost of registered childcare has been available since 2001 through a childcare tax credit element in the Working Families Tax Credit. However, parents still have to pay at least 30% of the fees, which they may find hard to afford on low wages, so that the impact of the tax credit is limited (Daycare Trust, 2001).

The quality of childcare services is an important consideration for parents (LaValle et al, 2000). Cases of poor supervision or even abuse by childcare providers, although rare, are understandably alarming to parents. Mainly on grounds of cost and convenience, the majority of employed British mothers (62%) use a partner or other relative to mind their children, while a further 13% use a friend or neighbour (FPSC, 1998). Only a quarter pay for formal childcare: 15% use a childminder, 6% a day nursery, 6% a nanny and 2% a workplace nursery. However, among employed women with a child under age five, over half pay for formal childcare, indicating that informal sources are less able to cope with the needs of pre-school children. Among graduate mothers of a child aged under five, less than 30% are employed full time and the proportions are even lower for less qualified mothers (see Chapter Five). Mothers of school-age children often restrict their employment to fit in with school hours and term times (37%) or work from home (6%). With 13 weeks of school holidays and most holiday play schemes operating for only a few weeks and for limited hours, it is not surprising that mothers of school-age children find full-time employment difficult to manage unless they can obtain informal childcare or afford to pay a childminder.

Family care commitments, combined with the lack of affordable high-quality care services in Britain, help to explain why much of the increase in women's employment has been in part-time employment of married women (Hakim, 1993). The disruptive effect of domestic and other caring responsibilities on women's employment histories, combined with gender discrimination in employment, has led to women having different kinds of jobs from men, lower pay and shorter working hours (Joshi, 1991). On return to the labour market after having children, women tend to experience occupational downgrading (Dex, 1987; Jacobs, 1999). Longitudinal research has shown that a one-year gap in employment for women incurs a wage penalty of 16% on average, double the corresponding penalty on men (Gregg et al, 2000). The adverse effect on earnings is especially marked when the return is to a different employer and to part-time work, a pattern reflecting women's need to accommodate dual roles. Thus a career break to care for children can have far-reaching effects on women's earnings.

For lone parents in Britain, the obstacles to employment are multiplied. The majority, 60%, live in poverty, unable to improve their situation through employment because of lack of affordable childcare (CPAG, 1998) and the benefits poverty trap. Without a partner, the informal sources of childcare are limited. Yet the cost of formal childcare is often prohibitive, as there is no partner's income to help towards fees. Partnered mothers often return to part-time employment when their children reach school age. But for a lone parent this is unlikely to bring financial gain compared with claiming means-tested Income Support, especially if they would also lose Housing Benefit by taking a job. Despite this disincentive, just over 40% of lone parents are employed. However, a third of these earn wages below the poverty level and 80% of those who are employed part time earn below the Council of Europe's decency threshold (CPAG, 1998). Among 20 countries studied, Britain has one of the lowest full-time employment rates for lone mothers – 17% compared with 67% in France and 61% in Finland (Bradshaw et al, 1996).

As noted above, divorced women are protected in the basic state pension by derived rights (see Table 4.1), and after divorce those who have children are covered by Home Responsibilities Protection if they are not employed. However, the declining value of the basic pension means they face poverty in later life unless they can accumulate substantial private pension entitlements. The remainder of the chapter focuses on women who are divorced or separated, assessing the impact of their maternal status on their employment participation and private pension coverage and comparing with other women. A key question is the extent to which childcare commitments limit divorced and separated women's employment and hence ability to compensate through their own pension entitlements for the loss of sharing a husband's pension in retirement.

Divorced women and pensions

The number of divorces in England and Wales rose from 25,000 in 1961 to 145,000 in 1981 and peaked at 165,000 in 1993, falling back to 141,000 in 2000 (ONS, 2002d). If current rates persist, two couples in five will ultimately divorce (Shaw, 1999). The proportion of women divorced by age 40 has risen from 6% of those born in 1926 to 25% of those born in 1956 (ONS, 2000b). In Britain the median duration of marriage at divorce is about 10 years; one in three divorcees remarry within seven years, although the likelihood declines for women over 35 (Rake et al, 2000). Over 55% of divorces involve couples with children aged under 16 (ONS, 2000b).

Since 70% of divorced mothers receive no child maintenance (Marsh et al, 2001), the majority are solely responsible for household expenses including the cost of raising their children. In this situation private pension contributions are likely to be a low priority compared with other demands on finances. Missed years of contributions in the early years of the working life dramatically reduce the eventual pension. For an individual who contributes to a final salary scheme, a 10-year childrearing break reduces pension income by at least a quarter (Ginn and Arber, 2000c). But the loss is usually more than this due to lower earnings following a career break and to the fact that any preserved pensions from a previous job are indexed only to inflation, not to the rise in average earnings. Losses are even greater in defined contribution (DC) pension schemes (personal pensions, stakeholder pensions and a growing number of occupational pensions). For example, a 10-year break before joining a DC pension scheme with contributions at £50 per month could result in a pension loss of over £100 per week (Ginn and Arber, 2000c).

A woman's pension position can be transformed by divorce, since she simultaneously loses the possibility of sharing a husband's pension as his wife and of receiving a survivor's pension as a widow. Qualitative research found that almost all divorced women interviewed were aware of this, yet half said their husband's pension was not taken into account in the divorce settlement. Many women divorce without any financial settlement in court. As one said: "I had no divorce settlement. He asked me for money" (PRA/HtA, 1997, p 31). The trauma of divorce makes it difficult to think about pensions at the time, even for the minority of women who consult a solicitor. One divorced woman explained: "At the time of divorce I was too upset and unwell to think clearly ... when I saw my solicitor." (PRA/HtA, 1997, p 31).

The 1999 Welfare Reform and Pensions Act introduced the potential to share pensions between spouses divorcing after December 2000. This represents a welcome recognition of the difficulties divorced women, like other lone parents, face in making financial provision for later life. However, pension disadvantages suffered by divorced women may still not be addressed or adequately remedied by the new law. Moreover, the new law will provide no relief for women whose cohabiting partnership breaks down and who suffer many of the same problems as divorcing women.

Research using the General Household Survey (GHS) is used to illustrate the pension prospects of British divorced women (Ginn and Price, 2002). The GHS provides information about a nationally representative sample of nearly 17,000 women aged between 20 and 59 and over 9000 aged over 65 living in private households in Britain, for three years combined (1994, 1995, 1996). In the analysis, divorced and separated women were combined, because of the small number of separated women, and referred to as 'divorced'. Employment was divided into full time (31 or more hours per week) and part time. Four categories of maternal status were distinguished: women who had never had a child; those who no longer had any children aged under 16 at home; those whose youngest child was aged 10-15; and those whose youngest child was aged under 10. The category 'never had child' includes both young women who may later have children and those who are past their reproductive age. First, the financial situation of older divorced women is outlined.

Older divorced women's income

Among women aged over 65, divorced women represented about 5% in the mid-1990s, although by 2011 the proportion of women projected to be divorced among those aged 65-74 is over 13%, rising to nearly 18% by 2021 (Shaw, 1999).

Divorced women have lower personal incomes, on average, than single or widowed women (see Chapter One, Figure 1.1). Poverty is particularly common among older divorced women, with 37% claiming means-tested Income Support in later life, compared with 24% of widows and 15% of single women (Ginn and Price, 2002). Among divorced older men, 17% claim Income Support. Divorced older women's low income arises mainly from lack of second tier pension income, especially occupational pensions. They are considerably worse off than divorced older men. While 30% of divorced and separated women over 65 had a private pension, with median receipts of £34 per week, 53% of divorced and separated men over 65 had a private pension, with median receipts of £46 per week (see Chapter One, Figure 1.2). Divorced women's income disadvantage in later life can be seen as a result of falling between two stools. Their ability to build their own pensions has been less than that of single women, but they have lost the opportunity to acquire a widow's pension based on any private pension entitlements of their deceased husband.

There has been increasing awareness among policy makers of divorced women's risk of poverty in later life, reflected in recent legislation to facilitate transfer of pension assets between divorcing spouses. This is discussed in the next section.

Divorce and finance: the legislative background since 1970

Since the 1973 Matrimonial Causes Act, judges have had discretion to apportion assets and income between spouses. The court's first consideration must be the welfare of any child aged under 18, so that priority is given to housing for the main carer, usually the mother, and her children. Among couples who consulted a solicitor, orders involving pension assets were rare, despite considerable evidence of disparity between divorcing husbands and wives in the amount of accrued pension entitlements (Field, 2000). Instead, pension rights were usually offset against other assets such as the house.

The trend towards a clean break policy in divorce settlements – cessation of maintenance for the divorced wife – led in the 1980s to increasing dissatisfaction among middle class divorced women facing an impoverished retirement. Moreover, research on the Australian and Scottish experiences showed women to be seriously disadvantaged by 'clean break' settlements (FPSC, 1999). The 1995 Pensions Act required courts to consider pension assets in financial settlements on divorce, even if retirement was distant. The Act permitted some or all of the pension lump sum or annuity to be 'earmarked' for the spouse of the pension scheme member and paid at the time of his retirement. However, earmarking provisions were rarely used. Earmarking has the drawback that it leaves most divorcing wives with no pension rights of their own: they depend on their husbands remaining alive, retiring and continuing to make payments. In four and a half years, under 2000 earmarking orders were made by courts – less than 0.3% of divorces (Eversheds, 2000).

The Labour government elected in 1997 took the matter forward and the 1999 Welfare Reform and Pensions Act containing the new 'pension sharing' provisions was passed and brought into force on 1 December 2000. Those petitioning for divorce are now entitled to argue for a share of their spouse's pension. This includes entitlements to occupational, personal and state second tier pensions (SERPS and State Second Pension) accumulated at the time of divorce. If the claim is successful, the entitlements are split between the divorcing spouses. However, there is no requirement to consider the difficulties divorced women with children are likely to have in building their own pension rights through earnings after divorce. For those divorcing in their twenties and thirties, there may be very little pension entitlement to share. Most younger divorced women continue to shoulder the main responsibility for childcare, restricting their employment. For women divorcing in midlife there is likely to be a larger pension entitlement to share, and with less constraint arising from childcare they are better able to work full time and improve their pension position. On the other hand, they have limited time in which to do so. Thus pension-sharing legislation may bring only limited improvements in divorced women's retirement income.

Divorced women's employment in relation to age, marital and maternal status

Since it is full-time employment which is most important for pension building (Ginn and Arber, 1996, 2002), the proportion employed full time is shown in Figure 4.3, by five-year age groups, for divorced, married, cohabiting and single women. Divorced women aged under 30 were less likely to be employed full time than other women – only 22%. However, after age 45 divorced women's full-time employment rate rose to over 40%, overtaking married and widowed women but lagging behind single and cohabiting women.

As discussed earlier in this chapter, a major reason for the low employment participation of lone mothers is the need to care for their children. Figure 4.4 shows the proportion of women in each marital status who have ever had children and the age of the youngest. Widows are excluded, since numbers were too few. The profile of divorced women according to maternal status is almost identical to that of married women. For both these groups of women, a third had at least one child aged under 10, some 16% had a youngest child aged 10-15 and a third had children who had either left home or were no longer dependent – that is, they no longer had any children aged under 16 at home. Only 12-14% were childless. Cohabiting women were almost equally likely to have a youngest child aged under 10, but were less likely than married or divorced women to have a child aged over 10 – only a fifth.

Figure 4.3: Percentage of women employed full time by age group and marital status

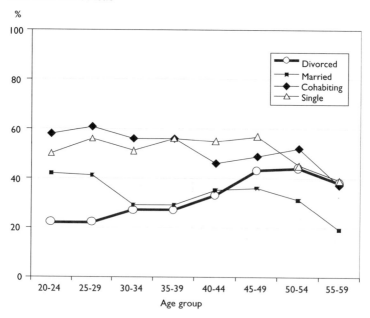

Source: Ginn and Price (2002), using data from the GHS, 1994-96

Figure 4.4: Percentage in each maternal category by marital status, women aged 20-59

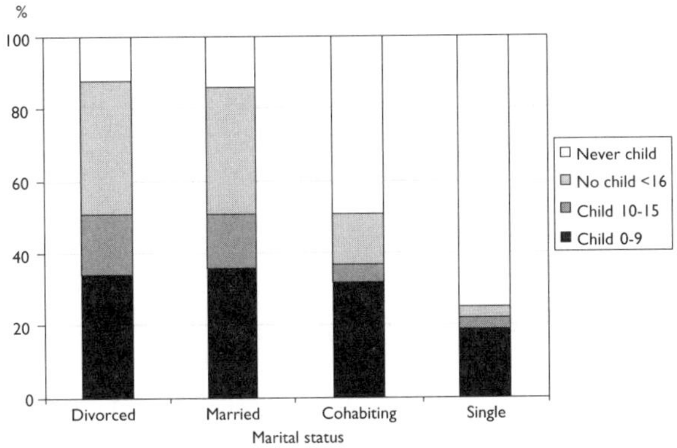

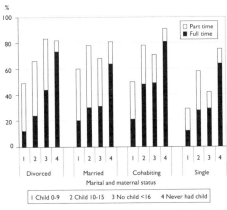

Source: Ginn and Price (2002), using data from the GHS, 1994-96

Figure 4.5 shows the relationship between maternal status and employment participation, for women in each marital status. Although all mothers show much lower full-time employment relative to childless women, the difference is more acute for lone than for partnered women. For example, nearly three quarters of childless divorced women worked full time, compared with only 12% of those with a child aged 0-9, 24% with a child aged 10-15 and 44% where children were no longer dependent. Significantly, among mothers with children aged under 16, married and cohabiting women had higher rates of full-time employment than divorced or single women. However, for childless women and those with children aged over 16, divorced women were more likely than married women to be employed full time.

Figure 4.5: Percentage employed full and part time by marital and maternal status, women aged 20-59

Source: Ginn and Price (2002), using data from the GHS, 1994-96

These results reflect the greater difficulty of lone mothers in taking a full-time job, compared with partnered mothers, but also suggest that, as childcare responsibilities become less onerous, divorced mothers make more effort than married mothers to earn their own living. Curiously, other research has shown that divorced men are far less likely to be employed than married men, even though few provide day-to-day childcare (Price and Ginn, 2003). We next turn to the question of divorced women's private pension coverage.

Private pension coverage in relation to marital and maternal status

Among all adults aged 20-59, half were contributing to a private pension: 63% of men and 38% of women (see Table 2.1). Among employees, membership of an occupational pension scheme rises with age, reaching its maximum for men in their forties and for women employed full time in their fifties, but remaining low for women part timers of all ages. In contrast, for personal pensions, peak coverage of full-time employees is in their thirties. These age effects need to be borne in mind since marital status is also associated with age, single women being younger than other groups of women.

Figure 4.6 shows the proportion of women contributing to a private (occupational or personal) pension by marital and maternal status. Overall, a third of divorced women had private pension coverage, somewhat less than among married women, 39%. Among childless divorced women 63% had pension coverage, but among divorced mothers of young children only 17% did so. Married mothers of children aged under 10 were twice as likely to contribute to a pension as similar divorced mothers. Even where children

Figure 4.6: Percentage contributing to a private pension by marital and maternal status, women aged 20-59

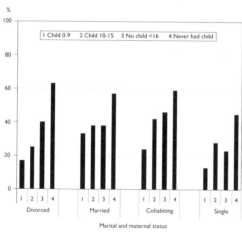

Source: Ginn and Price (2002), using data from the GHS, 1994-96

were aged 10-15, only a quarter of divorced mothers contributed to a private pension, again a much lower proportion than for equivalent married mothers.

In summary, the combination of being divorced and having dependent children reduces women's private pension coverage, mainly through the impact of childcare responsibilities on full-time employment. Moreover, other research has shown that divorced women are disadvantaged relative to other women in terms of the type of pension scheme and the level of contributions, that is, whether the minimum amount required is paid or whether an additional voluntary amount is paid (Price and Ginn, 2003). Thus divorced women's pension poverty is even more acute than is indicated simply by the rate of private pension coverage.

It is useful to summarise relevant differences between divorced men and women (see Table 4.2). Among divorced women in their twenties, over four fifths had at least one child aged under 10 at home, as did 57% of divorced women in their thirties. Accordingly, for divorced women aged under 40, rates of full-time employment and pension coverage were under half that of divorced men and on average their earnings were only a third of men's. These differences between divorced men and women became less dramatic over age 40, yet the employment and earnings gaps remained substantial for those in their forties and divorced women's disadvantage persisted into their fifties. Thus the disparity between the pension prospects of divorced men and women, if pension transfers towards women are not increased, is clear. Moreover, working age divorced women were less likely to be owner-occupiers (49%) than similar men (55%), compounding women's pension disadvantage. Divorced men were more likely both to own a house and contribute to a private pension (36%) than were divorced women (25%).

Table 4.2: A comparison of divorced women's and men's circumstances by age group

	Time since divorce, years		Child <10 %	Employed FT %		Earnings[a] £/week		Private pension %	
	Women	N	Women	Women	Men	Women	Men	Women	Men
All	9.5	1,322	34	33	62	£106	£217	32	49
20s	2.8	107	81	22	59	£60	£175	20	52
30s	6.2	412	57	27	72	£94	£256	26	55
40s	10.7	476	14	38	64	£124	£228	39	52
50s	14.2	327	1	42	50	£126	£180	38	40
N =		1,322[b]	1,912	1,912	991	1,912	991	1,912	991

Notes: [a] Median gross earnings, including those with zero earnings. [b] Not all divorced women reported age at first divorce.

Source: Ginn and Price (2002), using data from the GHS 1994-96

Summary and conclusions

The pension disadvantage of older divorced women is likely to be repeated as later cohorts of divorced women retire. Moreover, the proportion of older women who are divorced is projected to rise rapidly in the next 20 years. Among working age divorced individuals, women are half as likely to work full time as men, have only half men's median earnings and have substantially lower private pension coverage. Divorcees of working age are, of course, a diverse group, differentiated by educational qualifications and occupational experience at the time of divorce and, as our analysis highlights, by whether they have had children. While childless divorced women are able to build their own pensions just as well as childless single women, divorced mothers of dependent children have even lower private pension coverage than married mothers. Although divorced women's rates of full-time employment and pension coverage rise to exceed those of married women once their children are aged over 16, earnings and pension contributions are lost during the years of lone childrearing. As a result, most divorced women who have had children face a high risk of poverty and dependence on means-tested benefits in later life.

This research indicates both the need and the scope for pension transfers from ex-husbands to ex-wives through the 1999 Pensions and Welfare Act. However, despite misleading media reports, the Act does not give divorcing women the right to a share of their husband's pension, only the right to argue they should have such a share as part of an overall financial settlement – a very different thing. For owner-occupier couples, past practice has been to allow divorcing mothers to keep the family home while husbands keep their pensions, which are often crudely seen as of comparable value. Since the housing needs of children in the years following divorce will remain a priority, the practice of offsetting home against pension may continue, limiting the effectiveness of the legislation in protecting divorced women from poverty-level incomes in retirement (Price, 2003).

Even if divorced women with children were routinely awarded half of their husband's pension entitlement at the date of divorce, which would certainly help, substantial disparities in retirement income would remain between ex-spouses. While men are able to earn and accumulate a good pension after the divorce, the constraints on the divorced mother's employment and pension building continue. An equitable divorce settlement should take account of the longer term effects of motherhood in reducing earning capacity, and the fact that a money purchase pension started only in midlife has insufficient time to mature into a reasonable pension.

Pension sharing at divorce is not a panacea for the problem of later life poverty for divorced women. Nor does it help single mothers or cohabitees experiencing partnership breakdown. Even widows may be in a precarious position, despite rights to derived benefits from their deceased husband's second tier pension scheme. Not all husbands have a substantial pension to bequeath and widows only receive a fraction of the pension. For these disparate groups of women, pension disadvantage arises mainly from their role as mothers, in the context of a pension system designed for full-time continuous employment.

Changes in family formation and dissolution make it urgent to reconsider the appropriateness of derived benefits as a means of providing retirement income to those who have raised children. Derived benefits are neither adequate nor equitable as a means of compensating for the pension losses due to childrearing. If society values the work of raising children and caring for frail older family members, a means must be found to ensure that mothers do not pay a pension penalty. An 'independence model' of pensions would replace derived benefits with carer protection in state pensions, thus redistributing resources towards those whose earnings have been reduced by caring for others, irrespective of their marital status. Since the private sector of pensions is ill-adapted to achieve this, revitalising state pensions so that they provide an income well above poverty level is essential to this model.

Chapter Five examines how the impact of motherhood on pensions varies with human capital and assesses how far women's increasing educational qualifications may solve their pensions problem.

Impact of motherhood on pension acquisition: differentiation according to education

The effect of raising children on British women's employment, earnings and pension prospects was examined in Chapter Four, distinguishing according to partnership status. The analysis confirmed major divisions among women – between the child-free and those with dependent children and between partnered and lone mothers. Yet within these groups, women are further divided in terms of their human capital. Researchers have found a polarisation in British mothers' employment, in which those with high educational qualifications and occupational experience are able to buy childcare services and further their career, whereas others are constrained in their employment options by low earning power and unaffordable childcare.

British women's increasing levels of educational attainment have led to expectations of gender convergence in employment patterns and hence in lifetime earnings and pension income. As a growing proportion of women obtain graduate-level qualifications, they can expect to earn wages high enough to afford comprehensive childcare services. It is supposed that they will be able to maintain full-time employment after childbirth and maternity leave, matching men's traditional pattern of full-time continuous employment. Thus, according to an important and influential Cabinet Office publication (Rake et al, 2000), the 'motherhood gap' in pensions – the difference between a childless woman and a comparable mother – will in future be negligible for young women with a degree or equivalent qualification. This conclusion echoes the finding of a computer-simulation exercise by Davies et al (2000), which indicated that for women with high educational qualifications motherhood would typically incur no pension loss, as their employment would be almost continuously full time across their reproductive years. These authors suggest that for a typical graduate mother "employment is hardly perturbed by bearing two children", and that "part-time employment is limited for the mid-educated and negligible for graduates" (Davies et al, 2000, p 297). Rake et al (2000, p 85), drawing on these computer simulation results, conclude that the effects of child bearing are minimal for graduate women: "High-skilled mothers of two are estimated to remain continuously employed, with one year of part-time work following the birth of their second child."

The simulation exercise by Davies et al (2000) is valuable in illustrating the consequences of motherhood for women's incomes in later life and how these are likely to vary with educational level. The simulations were not intended to reflect average or representative women, but to provide typical scenarios. Nevertheless, the widely reported findings have been influential in conveying an optimistic message: that as the proportion of graduate women rises from the current 20%, a diminishing proportion of women will experience pension penalties due to motherhood and hence the need for redistributive state pensions and derived benefits in private pensions will recede.

This chapter reports research that assesses how realistic this message is. Data from the General Household Survey (GHS) was used to analyse the impact of motherhood on employment, earnings and private pension coverage according to women's educational qualifications. In particular, the claim that graduate mothers can expect negligible pension loss was critically examined (Ginn and Arber, 2002). A cross-sectional picture of women's employment, earnings and private pension coverage in the mid-1990s cannot predict pension entitlements at retirement since many of those not currently contributing to a private pension may have done so in the past and may do so in the future. Nevertheless there is a reasonably close correspondence between the cross-sectional gender difference in occupational pension scheme membership, where women's coverage rate is 63% of men's (Ginn and Arber, 2000a) and the gender difference in duration of membership, where women have 67% of men's membership duration. Among Britons aged over 60, men had typically contributed to an occupational pension scheme for 24 years, women for 16; similarly, among working-age men the average duration of membership was 15 years, but only 10 for women (Walker et al, 2000). This gives some confidence that analysis of cross-sectional data can give an indication of relative duration of coverage between different population groups, including the likely differentials in pension outcomes between childless women and those who ever had children.

Before presenting the findings concerning the impact of motherhood on women's pension prospects, it is useful to consider how and why women's employment participation is related to their educational level.

Women's employment and educational level

Among all women aged 20-59, those with higher education are much more likely to be employed than women with no qualifications, but the relationship is stronger among younger than older women (see Figure 5.1). This interaction between age and educational level in influencing women's employment participation is likely to reflect the tendency for more highly educated women to postpone childbearing until a later age than less skilled women, to take shorter career breaks for childrearing and to have a higher rate of childlessness (Beets, 1999).

Among employees, the proportion of men and women contributing to a private (occupational or personal) pension is related to educational level (Ginn and Arber, 2002). Graduates show a clear advantage in pension coverage over the less qualified, among both women and men and according to women's

Figure 5.1: Percentage of women employed, by age group and educational qualifications

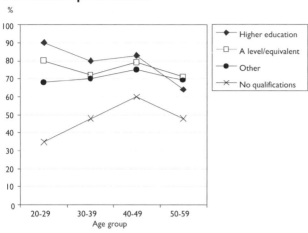

Source: Adapted from ONS (1998, Table 7.6)

hours of work. The gender difference in pension coverage was small among full-time employed graduates, but was larger at lower educational levels (Figure 5.2 and Appendix Table A5.1). However, women graduates employed part time were no more likely to have private pension cover (57%) than women full-timers with no qualifications (59%). This highlights the fact that, even for the most highly qualified women, working part time severely reduces the chance of contributing to a private pension scheme.

Figure 5.2: Percentage contributing to a private pension by educational level and hours of work, women employees aged 20-59

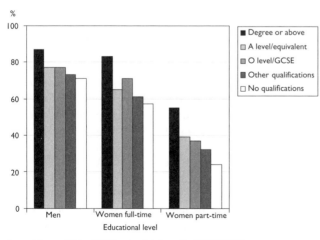

Source: Ginn and Price (2002), using data from the GHS 1994-96

Women's periods of part-time working and gaps in employment due to childrearing are becoming shorter and there has been a dramatic rise in the proportion of mothers who return to full-time employment within a year of childbirth – 5% in 1979 but 24% in 1996 (McRae, submitted 2002). The increase in maternal employment is most marked among those who are white, older, have fewer children and have educational qualifications (Brannen, 1999). Research has shown that for highly qualified young mothers, return to employment after childbearing is more rapid than for the less qualified (McRae, 1993; Dex et al, 1996). Glover and Arber (1995) showed a differentiation according to occupational class in terms of the length of gaps in employment when children were young. Moreover, the rate of full-time employment rose more rapidly with the age of the youngest pre-school child among women in higher non-manual occupations than among women in manual occupations. Nearly half of professional mothers were employed full time when their youngest child was aged 5-11 years compared with a fifth of mothers in manual jobs (Glover and Arber, 1995). However, recent longitudinal research shows that only a distinctive minority (10%) of mothers, mainly in professional or managerial jobs, maintained full-time employment continuously for 11 years after the birth of their first child, the majority having a mixture of full-time and part-time jobs with periods of non-employment (McRae, submitted 2002).

There are several reasons why qualifications mediate the impact of having children on participation in employment. First, rapid return to full-time employment in the same job is easier for well-qualified women. This is particularly so for women who postpone childbearing until they have established themselves in a professional or managerial occupation. For the majority of women the strategy of using all-day childcare is less available because their earnings are too low (Ward et al, 1996). Second, having a well-qualified partner further reduces the impact of motherhood. Homogamous partnering, in which men and women of similar educational level tend to marry or cohabit, reinforces differentials in household income and hence in capacity to pay for childcare. Third, highly qualified women tend to occupy jobs that provide better employment rights, such as relatively long maternity leave with pay, as well as family-friendly arrangements for return to the same job after childbearing (Glover and Arber, 1995). Fourth, the low wages associated with low qualifications do not encourage women back into the labour market. Even where lack of childcare is not a barrier to employment, the financial gain after paying for childcare will be very limited if earnings are low. In this situation it is not surprising that many women with low qualifications opt to care for their own pre-school children and to take a part-time, term-time job once their children are at school. As noted in Chapter Four, lone mothers are less likely than partnered mothers to be able to return quickly to full-time employment.

Thus in Britain returner patterns vary according to human capital, with a "small group of mothers with considerable educational and occupational capital and a much larger group of mothers without such capital" (Glover and Arber,

1995, p 169). This differentiation of returner patterns according to qualifications magnifies the pre-existing occupational pay differentials among women (Dex et al, 1996). Women whose educational qualifications enable them to return after childbearing to full-time employment in the same job can maintain or improve their occupational status. In contrast, those who return to part-time employment after a period of childrearing often take a different job and typically suffer downward occupational mobility (Dex et al, 1996).

The variation in women's employment patterns according to their level of qualifications suggests a similar differentiation in pension prospects, exacerbated by the current shift in the balance of pension provision towards private pensions. While highly qualified women may begin to match men's private pension income in later life (as single, childless women have done in the past, see Ginn and Arber, 1991) the pension outlook for women who have periods of part-time employment to accommodate family needs is less rosy. Part-timers are less likely to contribute to a private pension and, if they do, their lower earnings lead to a lower pension. Although low earnings early in the lifecourse have no direct effect on final salary occupational pensions, employers are increasingly switching to defined contribution (or money purchase) schemes (see Chapter One). In such schemes, the pension is reduced by periods of low earnings, especially if these occur early in the working life. Low earnings will have a similarly detrimental effect on personal (including stakeholder) pensions, compounded by the fact that employers generally make no contributions to these pensions.

In the remainder of this chapter, research is presented on the relationship between women's lifecourse stage and their employment and private pension coverage, distinguishing according to their human capital in terms of educational level (Ginn and Arber, 2002). To what extent can qualifications protect women from the impact of motherhood on their private pension acquisition?

To address this question, data from three years combined (1994-96) of the GHS were used. Women were grouped according to their highest educational qualification into five categories: degree/equivalent or above, A levels, O levels/GCSE, other qualifications and no qualifications. Full-time employment included all those whose usual hours of work were at least 31 per week, whether employees or self-employed. Membership of private pensions includes occupational and personal pensions (including personal pensions for the self-employed). Women were grouped into six categories, in order distinguish successive stages in the lifecourse:

1. those aged under 35 who had never borne a child;
2. those with a youngest child aged 0-4 in the family;
3. those with a youngest child aged 5-9 in the family;
4. those with a youngest child aged 10-15 in the family;
5. those who had borne a child but had no child aged under 16 in the family;
6. those aged over 35 who had never borne a child.

Among women aged under 35 who had never had a child, roughly three quarters can be expected to pass through the four stages of motherhood, while a quarter can be expected to remain childless, moving straight from category 1 to 6. Women aged under 35 were born after 1960 and entered the labour market between 1980 and 1995, so their employment fully reflects the momentous changes of the 1970s in equality legislation, educational opportunities and attitudes towards sex equality and women's roles – the 'new gender settlement' (Walby, 1999). Therefore certain analyses were restricted to women aged under 35, comparing childless women with mothers of young children while controlling for educational level. This indicates the differences in employment and pension coverage associated with motherhood within this late cohort. The mean ages of childless women and mothers aged under 35 were not very different, 26.3 and 28.5 years old.

Lifecourse stage and women's employment

Women's rates of employment and of full-time employment differed according to maternal status and age group (Figure 5.3). However, women's total employment rates were less affected by maternal responsibilities than their full-time rates, since part-time employment can often be accommodated (Figure 5.3a). The employment rate of childless women and women with children aged over 10 was high among those in their forties but fell to only 50% among all women in their late fifties, a key age for pension building. Reduced employment among those with children aged from 0-4 was more marked for women aged under 30 than for those in their thirties and forties.

Full-time employment, in contrast, was reduced considerably for women with childcare responsibilities (Figure 5.3b). Among mothers of children aged under 10, under a fifth were employed full time at all ages. The full-time employment rate was still under a third for all age groups of women with children aged 10-15 and was under half where women had children aged 16 and over. Full-time employment of childless women peaked among those in their late twenties at 80%, declining thereafter, more steeply from the late forties to only 40% in the early fifties, and under 30% in the late fifties. Very few women in their fifties were in full-time employment, an employment position that would help to maximise their pension accumulation. For married women in this older cohort, this may reflect a norm of non-employment or secondary wage earning (in which a wife's wages are a necessary but minor supplement to the household income).

Figure 5.3: Percentage of women employed by maternal status and age group

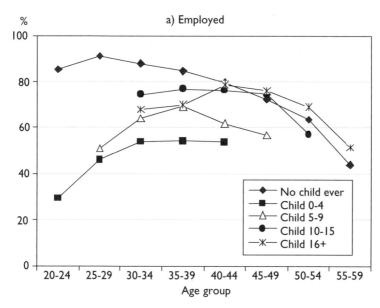

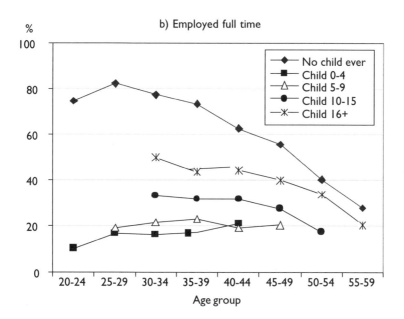

Source: Ginn and Arber (2002), using data from the GHS 1994-96

Figure 5.4: Percentage employed by lifecourse category and education level, women aged 20-59

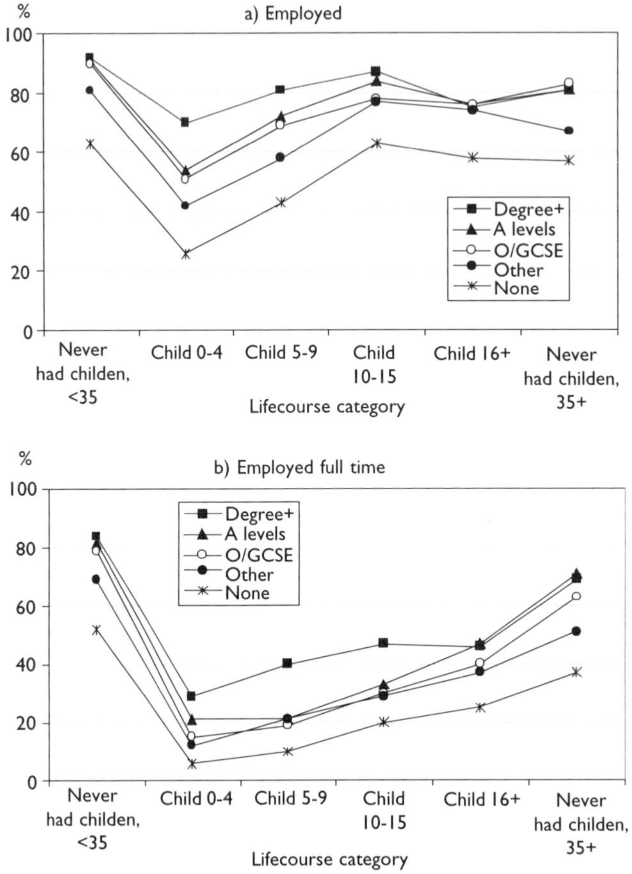

Source: Ginn and Arber (2002), using data from the GHS 1994-96

In order to assess the effect of motherhood on the employment of women with different levels of qualifications, women's employment was analysed by lifecourse category, controlling for educational level (Figure 5.4 and Appendix Table A5.2). Since accumulating adequate private pension entitlements depends mainly on full-time employment, discussion will focus on this. Figure 5.4b shows a dramatic reduction in full-time employment among mothers in all educational groups. In each of the four stages of motherhood, under half of graduate women were employed full time and among those with children aged under five less than a third were in full-time employment. This casts doubt on the models of lifetime earnings and pensions of graduate mothers estimated by Davies et al (2000) and Rake et al (2000), and suggests graduate mothers' losses may have been seriously underestimated.

The impact of having children varied according to educational level. For example, the proportion of mid-skilled women (with O levels/GCSE) who were employed full time was 79% among those who were childless and aged under 35, but was only 15% among those with a child under age five. For graduates, the equivalent proportions were 84% and 29%, still a substantial difference. The strongest association between motherhood and reduced full employment was for women with O levels/GCSE (see Table A5.2).

In sum, the effect of having young children at home on women's likelihood of being employed full time was substantial at all educational levels, although less for graduates than for less qualified women.

Lifecourse stage and women's earnings

Both lack of earnings and low pay adversely affect private pension building. Measuring the average earnings of all working-age women, including those not employed, indicates the effect of motherhood on the eventual amount of a woman's private pension, if any. Mothers had substantially lower median earnings than childless women (Figure 5.5 and Appendix Table A5.3, last column). Median weekly earnings were zero for those with a youngest child aged under five and £42 for those with a youngest child aged 5-9, £80 for those with a youngest child aged 10-15, £69 for those with no children under 16 at home, compared with £196 and £162 for the two age groups of childless women (under 35 and over 35 respectively). Thus median earnings of mothers of children aged 5-9 were only 21% of those of childless women aged under 35, while the proportion rose to 41% for mothers of older dependent children. Compared with the

Figure 5.5: Median earnings by lifecourse category and educational level, women aged 20-59

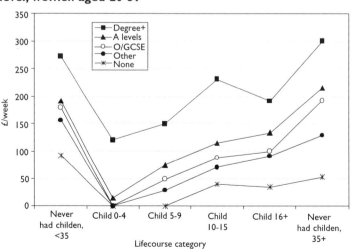

Source: Ginn and Arber (2002), using data from the GHS 1994-96

median earnings of all men aged 20-59 (£250 per week), mothers of children aged 5-9 earned on average only 17%. The earnings of mothers of the youngest children, aged from 0-4, were an even smaller proportion of the earnings of childless women or men.

Although graduates maintained higher earnings across all lifestage categories, as would be expected, even these highly skilled mothers experienced an initial fall in earnings to less than half that of childless graduates, on average (see Figure 5.5). The median weekly wage of childless graduates aged under 35 was £272, compared with £120 for graduate mothers of children aged up to four, reducing potential current pension contributions. The earnings of graduate mothers 'recovered' after the first two stages of motherhood, on average to £231 per week when children were aged 10-15 but 'fell' again to £191 among those whose children were all aged over 16; this fall may be an age cohort effect, since many graduates with children aged over 16 were in their fifties, an age group with a lower employment rate (see Figure 5.2). The highest median earnings were received by childless graduates aged over 35, £300 per week. Thus, even for graduates, the lifetime earnings of mothers are likely to be substantially less than for childless women.

The analysis so far has shown that obtaining a degree, while increasing women's chance of full-time employment and high earnings, does not allow women to escape the adverse effects of motherhood on full-time employment and earnings. In the next section, the effect of motherhood on private pension coverage is analysed according to educational level.

Private pension coverage

Private (occupational and personal) pension coverage of working age adults represents the outcome of many labour market factors, including their employment participation, hours of work and employment status (employee or self-employed). Figure 5.6 (and Appendix Table A5.4) shows private pension coverage according to age group and maternal status for all women aged 20-59, including those not currently employed. Among women who had had a child, pension coverage only exceeded 40% among those aged over 40 whose youngest child was aged over 16, whereas childless women had much higher coverage. However, childless women had declining pension coverage rates over age 40, reflecting lower full-time employment rates in older cohorts (see Figure 5.3b).

The relationship between women's lifecourse category and private pension cover is shown for each educational group in Figure 5.7 (and Appendix Table A5.5). As expected, in each lifecourse category those with the highest qualifications were most likely to contribute to a private pension and at each educational level childless women had higher coverage rates than women who had had children. For example, among graduate women over two thirds of those who were childless (65% of those under 35, 72% over 35) contributed to a private pension, compared with about 55% of mothers of young children. The impact of lifecourse category on private pension coverage was least for

Figure 5.6: Percentage contributing to a private pension by maternal status and age group, women aged 20-59

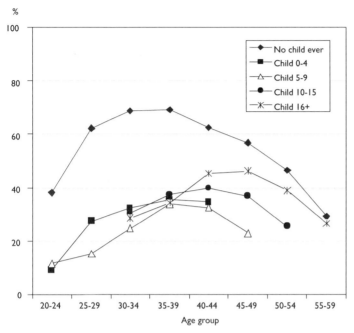

Source: Ginn and Arber (2002), using data from the GHS 1994-96

Figure 5.7: Percentage contributing to a private pension by lifecourse category and educational level, women aged 20-59

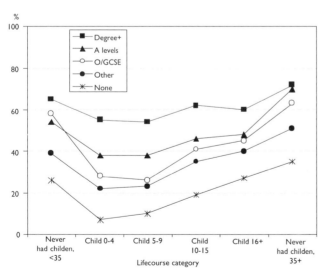

Source: Ginn and Arber (2002), using data from the GHS 1994-96

graduates and greatest for those with mid-level qualifications, O level/GCSE, while the effect was intermediate for the remaining three educational groups. A similar pattern applied when the analysis was restricted to the youngest cohort, women aged under 35. Motherhood had the greatest effect among mid-skilled women, reducing pension coverage by over half, from 58% to 27%.

This analysis has shown that the impact of motherhood on private pension coverage is less dramatic than the effect on full-time employment and earnings, reflecting pension scheme contributions made by women in part-time jobs. However, contributions made on reduced earnings are less valuable in terms of accumulating pension wealth. Taking this into account, the private pension loss among mothers, although less for graduates than for less qualified mothers, is likely to be substantial.

Summary and conclusions

Although the impact of motherhood on employment, earnings and private pension coverage is less for graduates than for other women, it is still far from negligible. Contrary to the conclusions of Davies et al (2000) and Rake et al (2000), there is no support for the expectation that graduate mothers will maintain almost continuous full-time employment throughout their lifecourse. Full-time employment was under a third for graduate mothers of pre-school children and remained below half for those with older children. This indicates that even graduate mothers take several years, on average, out of full-time employment. Since only a third of graduate mothers of children aged under 10 were employed full time, this implies that on average women with a degree lose nearly seven years of full-time employment while their children are young.

Pension coverage was reduced among graduates with a child aged under 10, from 65 to 55%. Further, among employed graduate mothers of a child aged under 10, the majority worked part time, reducing the amounts of pension contributions they could make even if they belonged to a private pension scheme. The halving of median earnings among graduate mothers of young children indicates the extent of the pension contribution loss for this group due to a combination of non-employment, part-time hours and occupational downgrading. In all, the analysis suggests that even graduate mothers will experience a substantial loss of private pension entitlements compared with their childless counterparts and that the pension-protective power of a degree for women has been overstated.

The impact of motherhood on pension prospects was much more serious for the majority of women without degree-level qualifications. Mid-skilled women (those with GCSEs or O levels) experienced the greatest loss in pension coverage due to childrearing, even though their level of coverage was higher than that of women with other or no qualifications.

The younger generation of women, aged under 35, are better qualified than women aged over 35, but the change has been mainly to increase the proportion of women with GCSE and A levels, while reducing the proportion with no

Figure 5.8: Percentage of women at each educational level by age group

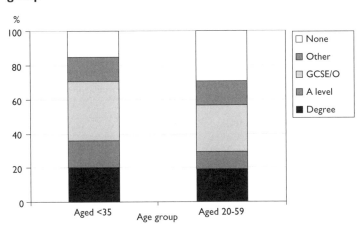

Source: Ginn and Arber (2002), using data from the GHS 1994-96

qualifications (see Figure 5.8). Since the mid-skilled group of women show a particularly strong association between motherhood and reduced employment, earnings and private pension coverage, a substantial pension loss is likely to continue for the majority of women who have children. This should be a matter of concern to policy makers, especially in view of the loosening link between motherhood and marriage, discussed in Chapter Four.

Policy towards women's dual roles of paid employment and family caring has in the past two decades shifted decisively towards promoting the employment of mothers, although in practice this is often part time. Women's greater opportunities in education and employment are welcome.

However, in seeking to facilitate women's greater participation in the labour market, we should not lose sight of the importance of ensuring mothers can make their own decisions about when the time is right for them to return to employment, leaving their children with others for part or all of the day. Raising children (and caring for older relatives) is as valuable as many occupations, more so than some. As Himmelweit (1998) has argued, the unpaid care economy and the paid economy are interdependent since the latter requires a healthy, educated workforce and a functioning society. The practical tasks and less tangible emotional work done in caring for children or for frail relatives promotes a form of welfare that is hard to measure yet is vital to the continuation of a civilised society (Fast et al, 1999). Workfare schemes in the US that require mothers to leave their children in the care of others in order to take a low paid job stem from a mistaken conceptualisation of caring for children at home as 'nonwork' (Grace, 1998). A similar argument is made by Fast et al (2001) in relation to care for older people. Transferring labour in this way from the care economy to the paid economy artificially inflates growth in the national economy (Cloud and Garrett, 1996), yet it is not costless and may be counter-productive.

"If insufficient time and resources are devoted to [unpaid care], productivity will suffer as human resources deteriorate and the social fabric is inadequately maintained" (Himmelweit, 1998, p 7).

If the role of mothers in caring for their children is valued as work, this implies protecting pension entitlements during periods of childcare, as is the case in state pensions in Britain and in many other European countries (see Chapter Six). However, the dominance of private pensions and meagre state pensions in Britain means that the proportion of pension entitlements protected in this way is small. Increasing policy emphasis on private pensions reinforces the pension penalties of motherhood. On the other hand, a basic state pension set at an adequate level could minimise such losses for working age women, as well as lifting out of poverty those older women whose pension building has been restricted by family caring commitments.

In Chapter Six, the way other EU countries meet the pension needs of those with childcare responsibilities is outlined.

SIX

Gender and pensions in the European Union: towards an independence model?

Key concerns of policy makers throughout the developed world are to ensure financial sustainability of state pension schemes without sacrificing adequacy of pensions to meet the needs of older people and future pensioners. Population ageing, which is partly due to falling fertility rates, has brought the question of sustainability of pensions into prominence, although whether this constitutes a serious problem, and in which countries, has been subject to debate (Walker, 1990; Mullan, 2000; Street and Ginn, 2001). Since the employment rate in the working age population is also important to the viability of any pension scheme (state or private) it is useful to consider the relationship between women's fertility and their employment. Is there an inevitable trade-off, for women, between social reproduction and economic production?

The chapter first considers the social value of unpaid care work and compares women's fertility and their employment across EU countries. Britain's pension system is then compared with those of other EU countries in terms of adequacy, gender inequality of later life income and the treatment of family caring. Finally, the question of moving towards an independence model of pensions is discussed.

The gendered lifecourse and social reproduction

The research reported in Chapters Four and Five focused on the impact of women's childcare commitments on their employment and pensions in the context of a lack of affordable childcare services in Britain. The government recognise that mothers find childcare a barrier to employment: "Women tell us that a key obstacle to their re-entering the labour market is accessing affordable and good quality childcare" (DWP, 2002, p 117), although it is not only childcare that conflicts with women's employment participation. Women over age 50 are often called upon to provide informal care for ageing parents or parents-in-law or to look after their grandchildren while their daughters or daughters-in-law engage in paid work.

The provision of family caring and consequences for employment and pension building are usually seen as problems solely for women. For practical reasons, earlier chapters of this book are based on the assumption that working age carers are usually women, neglecting those men who also devote time to family caring at the expense of their employment, earnings and pension rights. Given the increasing fluidity of family forms, it is timely to recall that gender denotes socially constructed roles and identities, and is not merely an alternative, politically correct, term for sex. In western countries a minority of women, mainly those who are childless or who are highly qualified partnered mothers, pursue a typically 'masculine' lifecourse in terms of continuity of full-time employment. Equally, a minority of men undertake caring tasks, either as lone fathers or through role reversal in which their partner is the main breadwinner while they interrupt their employment, following a typically 'feminine' lifecourse. Thus gender, in the limited but important sense of the distribution of paid and unpaid work roles over the lifecourse, is becoming less closely linked to sex and represents a spectrum of lifecourse patterns rather than a dichotomy. In the gendered lifecourse, the variation is between a more feminine or a more masculine pattern, not simply between men and women.

Unpaid family caring work is often conceived as a private matter of voluntary labour within the family. Yet it is crucial to the welfare and even survival of society – a point which is obvious but has generally been overlooked by economists. First, the care needs of the young, the sick and frail elderly individuals are unlikely to diminish. Parents' investment of time and energy in bearing, nurturing and socialising children, like informal care for older people, is labour-intensive, time-dependent, emotionally demanding and person-specific. Although marketised or statutory services are an important support to parents and other carers, they do not fully replace family care. The value of unpaid domestic labour to the economy (including other domestic work as well as caring) is gaining recognition among statisticians, with plans to measure and record unpaid work in national statistics. For example, the value of women's unpaid domestic work was estimated as £259 billion or 42% of GDP (calculated from Murgatroyd and Neuburger, 1997) – not a trivial contribution and one that reduces women's time for paid employment as well as engagement in civic, political and social life.

Second, falling birth rates have serious implications for societies, especially when fertility remains below the replacement rate (2.1 children per woman) over an extended period, an unprecedented development that is occurring in most OECD countries (Coleman, 2000). In the EU as a whole, the average total fertility rate in the 15 EU countries has nearly halved in 33 years, falling from 2.7 in 1960 to 1.4 in 1993. The shortfall in the birth rate, and the decline between successive birth cohorts of women, varies across countries (see Figure 6.1). In all EU countries except Ireland, women born in 1963 did not replace their generation – although the outcome is not yet entirely determined, due to the trend to later childbearing (Beets, 1999). Ireland, with the Mediterranean countries, had the steepest decline in fertility, while Denmark and Sweden's were stable and Luxembourg and Finland even showed a slight increase in fertility between the two cohorts.

The reasons for fertility trends over time and for cross-country variation are debated among demographers but are thought to relate less to cash benefits for parenthood than to other factors such as the domestic division of labour and

Figure 6.1: Completed fertility, generations of women born in 1950 and 1963 (EU15)

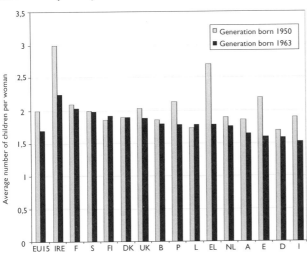

Note: For key to the EU15 countries, please see Table 6.3.

Source: Eurostat, Demographic Statistics, cited in Bagavos and Martin (2000)

family policies that enable women to combine employment and childrearing (Bagavos and Martin, 2000). Women in highly marketised societies need to earn an independent income and, in the absence of suitable policies to reconcile childrearing and employment, this creates pressure to delay or forgo childbearing: "The risk-averse woman of today will ensure that she is able to support herself and, given the chance of relationship breakdown, will be careful not to put herself in a position of dependency on a man" (McDonald, 2000). However, in countries with social policies to support childrearing – including adequate paid maternity and parental leave, availability of quality, subsidised daycare for children, after-school care, individual taxation and opportunities to shorten hours of work temporarily without changing jobs – the conflict between women's roles in reproduction and in production is less. Finland exemplifies such policies (Taskinen, 2000). It has been suggested that "fertility is higher in the member states where: the caring activities are better shared between men and women, public caring infrastructure is more developed, part-time jobs are more available, legislation is more family-friendly" (Eurostat, 2001, p 28). In the next section, trends in women's employment are compared among EU countries.

Comparing women's employment in EU countries

In the EU as a whole, 37% of working-age women are employed full time, with 14% working part time (under 30 hours a week). The figures for men are 67% and 4% respectively (OECD, 2001b). Women's rates of full-time employment range from the lowest levels in the Netherlands, Italy and Spain (27-30%), through medium levels in Britain, Ireland, Germany, France and Switzerland (36-41%) to the highest in Denmark and Sweden (55-57%).

Full-time employment rates of men and women are shown for eight EU countries, from 1990 to 2000, in Figure 6.2 (and Appendix Table A6.1). In 2000, a relatively high proportion of women (50-60%) were employed full time in Denmark and Sweden. This also applies in Finland (not shown). Italy and the Netherlands had low rates of full-time employment of women, under 30%, while the range was 35-41% in France, Britain, Germany and Ireland. Over the decade, the proportion of women employed full time rose substantially in Denmark, Ireland and the Netherlands, although from a low base in these latter two countries. The increase was very slight in France, Germany and Britain, while no rise was evident in Sweden and Italy. Part-time employment of women rose in all countries except Denmark and Sweden, while that of men rose slightly in seven of the countries (Table A 6.1).

Figure 6.2: Percentage employed full time, men and women in eight EU countries (1990-2000)

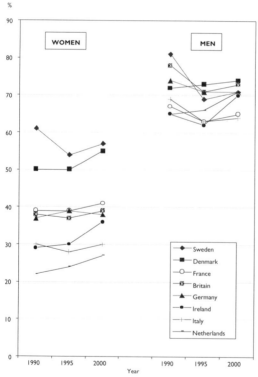

Notes: As a % of population aged 15-64 (16-64 in Britain and Sweden). Break in series after 1990 for Sweden, Denmark, Germany and Italy.

Source: Calculated from OECD (2000, 2001, Tables A and E)

Women's employment participation is related to their maternal status but the extent to which women reduce their hours of employment after giving birth varies among countries (Blossfeld and Hakim, 1997). This highlights the role of social structure, especially childcare provision and school hours, in influencing mothers' employment participation. The constraint on mothers' hours of work is more severe in Britain than in those European countries where affordable quality childcare services are widely available (Joshi and Davies, 1992). According to Esping-Andersen (1999), the net cost of childcare for two children under the age of three, as a proportion of average family income, was 9% in France, 11% in Denmark and the US, 16% in Sweden, 28% in the United Kingdom and 39% in Italy. The UK has the lowest level of publicly funded childcare provision for children aged under three in the EU and relatively short paid maternity and parental leave (Esping-Andersen, 2002).

The effect of motherhood on employment was demonstrated by Harkness and Waldfogel (1999) using Luxembourg Income Study data for women aged 24-44 in seven countries including Britain, Germany, Finland and Sweden. Mothers' employment participation was substantially less than that of childless women in each country, but the effect of children was greatest in Britain and negligible in Sweden. The 'family gap' was even more striking for full-time employment. For example, 76% of British women without children were employed full time compared with only 26% of women who had children, while the equivalent rates were 72 and 40% in Germany, 75 and 61% in Sweden and 79 and 66% in Finland (Harkness and Waldfogel, 1999).

The pay penalty of motherhood also varies among EU countries. Harkness and Waldfogel (1999) found that the 'family gap in pay' for women aged 24-44 (after taking account of age, education and other relevant variables) was substantial in Britain, rising from 8% for one child to 24% for two children. The wage penalty for two children was much less in other countries – 11% in Germany, 3% in Finland and only 1% in Sweden. These results are consistent with the finding of Gornick et al (1997) that social policies in three social democratic welfare states (Denmark, Sweden and Finland) facilitate women's dual roles in reproduction and production, whereas in three Anglophone welfare states (Britain, Australia and the US) women "faced stiff penalties for work absence due to childbirth; without publicly subsidised childcare many had few viable alternatives to full-time maternal care of children" (Gornick et al, 1997, p 64).

The quality of part-time jobs and the number of hours typically worked influence the impact of motherhood on pay, and these vary among EU countries (O'Reilly and Fagan, 1998). For example, in 1988, the average weekly hours worked by part-timers were 25 in Sweden but only 17 in Britain (Sainsbury, 1996, Table 5.3). Where hours are longer, part-time employment is less strongly linked to low pay, low occupational status and poor long-term prospects (Cousins, 1994). If part-time employment is possible in professional occupations and is used by employers as a way of retaining valued staff, it is more a bridge than a trap for women. For example, Swedish and Finnish mothers of young children have the statutory right to reduce their working week to 30 hours without loss of occupational status or hourly rate of pay. International variation in the quality of part-time jobs suggests that, although market forces tend to push the most vulnerable workers into the poorest jobs, state intervention can improve the quality of part-time employment. Despite British legislation in 2000, high-quality part-time jobs were still the exception rather than the rule in 2002 and hourly pay was much less than for full-timers.

Where a lack of family-friendly policies contributes to women typically having reduced lifetime earnings, the pension penalties vary with the structure of a country's pension system, especially the extent to which pensions are tied to earnings over the working life (Ginn and Arber, 1992). A key issue is how far EU pension systems have incorporated arrangements to enable those with family caring commitments to build adequate pension entitlements of their own (an independence model of pension provision) or instead rely mainly on carers receiving entitlements derived from their marital status (a male breadwinner model). The next section compares both the adequacy of EU pensions and their adaptations to fit the dual roles of women's paid and unpaid work – their carer-friendliness.

Comparing EU pension systems: adequacy and carer-friendliness

Adequacy

The European Council at its Laeken meeting in 2001 recorded agreement by member states on 11 objectives for pension systems, under the headings of adequacy, sustainability and modernisation to meet changing societal needs (EC, 2002). In terms of adequacy, member states are enjoined to:

1. ensure that older people are not placed at risk of poverty and can enjoy a decent standard of living; that they share in the economic well-being of their country and can accordingly participate actively in public, social and cultural life; and
2. provide access for all individuals to appropriate pension arrangements, public and/or private, which allow them to earn pension entitlements enabling them to maintain, to a reasonable degree, their living standard after retirement.

Older people in Britain are at a higher risk of poverty than in many other EU countries, according to the most recent poverty statistics for the EU. The poverty rate for individuals aged over 65 in 1998, using the EU definition of income below 60% of national median equivalised income, was 21% in Britain, compared with 11% in Germany, 8% in Sweden and 7% in the Netherlands (Figure 6.3 and Appendix Table A6.2a). British pensioners' median income was only 78% of that of the population aged under 65. This compares with a relative income for older people of over 90% in Germany, France, the Netherlands, Italy and Luxembourg (Figure 6.3 and Appendix Table A6.2b).

Figure 6.3: Poverty rates[a] and relative income[b] among those aged 65+ (EU15)

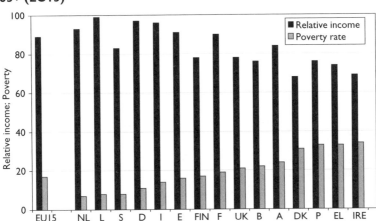

Notes: [a] Percentage aged 65+ with income less than 60% of the median equivalised income of the national population. [b] Median equivalised income of those aged 65+ as percentage of that of the population aged 0-64

For key to the EU15 countries, please see Table 6.3.

Source: CEC 2003, Table 2, based on European Community Household Panel Survey data for 1998

Earlier figures produced by Eurostat (2002) showed Britain to have the highest pensioner poverty rate among EU countries at 40%. However, these figures were reworked during 2002 at the insistence of the British government.

Not surprisingly, poverty measures are highly controversial. Comparisons of poverty across countries must be treated with caution due to inter-country variation in charges for services such as healthcare and in provision of other non-cash benefits. Statistics on poverty rates are affected by unreliable reporting of incomes and missing income data. Poverty rates are also sensitive to the assumptions made. In particular, the EU poverty measures, by taking combined household income and then assigning each individual an equal share adjusted for household size (that is, equivalising income), effectively underestimate the prevalence of personal poverty among women who live with a partner or other relative.

An alternative way of defining poverty (instead of relative to national population average) is in relation to the income required to pay for goods and services at a basic or a modest level. Research in Britain by the Family Budget Unit calculated the weekly income required to provide a basic – Low Cost but Acceptable (LCA) – living standard for people aged 65-74, in 1999 prices (Parker, 2000). The LCA amounts, uprated for earnings rises between 1999 and 2002, are shown in Table 6.1. For those aged over 75, the majority of whom are women, the amounts required would be higher to take account of disability and other health problems.

Over two million pensioners (mainly non-married women) are poor enough to receive the MIG and it is estimated that a further half a million more are

Table 6.1: Comparison of basic state pension and MIG with LCA amounts for people aged 65-74 (2002, £ per week)

| | Full basic pension | MIG | LCA amounts, uprated to 2002 | |
			LA tenants	Homeowners
Non-married person	75.50	98.15	141.00	115.00
Married couple[a]	120.80	149.80	210.00	170.00

Note: [a] Assuming husband has full pension and wife has 60%. Cohabiting women have no entitlement to a derived pension based on their partner's contribution record, but cohabiting and married couples receive the same MIG.

entitled but fail to claim (DSS, 1999). Despite government attempts to increase take-up of the MIG, this has proved an intractable problem (Corden, 1999; Evason et al, 2002). Since the LCA standard is substantially higher than the MIG, many more than 2.5 million pensioners are living below the LCA standard. According to the government's own figures, the proportion of pensioners at risk of poverty in the year 2000 was 31% of women and 25% of men, while the proportion among pensioner women living alone was as high as 46% (DSS, 2000).

Whichever measure of poverty is used, it is clear that a substantial proportion of British pensioners, mainly women, lack sufficient income to "participate actively in public, social and cultural life" and to "maintain, to a reasonable degree, their living standard after retirement". Despite using means testing to supplement meagre state pensions, British pension policy fails to satisfy EU objectives on adequacy and performs poorly compared with the EU as a whole. It is debatable whether this situation is acceptable in a rich country.

Carer-friendliness

Older women bear a disproportionate share of poverty throughout the EU, having lower personal incomes than older men, due mainly to smaller pensions (Dooghe and Appleton, 1995; Walker and Maltby, 1997). However, the magnitude of women's pension disadvantage varies across countries. As Walker and Maltby (1997) note, in the 1990s older women's pension income as a proportion of men's was approximately 66% in Italy, 56% in France and 42% in Germany. In Britain it was about 60%. This does not imply that older women in Germany are poorer than their British counterparts, but that gender inequality is more acute. In Denmark gender inequality of pension income was much less than in the rest of the EU (Walker et al, 1993), due to the dominant role of the residence-based citizen's pension.

Pension systems can be compared in terms of carer-friendliness – incorporation of features that help to redistribute towards those whose employment has been restricted by their family caring commitments. These features may be included in any of the three major sources of pension entitlements – state pension entitlements based on the individual's paid employment and unpaid caring work; state pension entitlements derived from relationship to a husband (alive and still married, divorced or deceased); and private pensions, including both occupational (DB or DC) and personal pensions (see Table 6.2). In contributory state pension schemes, gender differences in access to the pension and likely amount of entitlement depend on a number of design features of the pension scheme, such as whether there are earnings or hours thresholds for access, whether there is some form of carer credit and how the amount of pension is determined (Table 6.2a). Citizen's pensions, although often referred to as

Table 6.2: Key components of pension systems from a gender perspective

a) State pensions (individual entitlement)

Access	Earnings or hours thresholds for contributions
	Years threshold for residence-based pension
	The treatment of years of caring
	Age for pension qualification
Amount	Whether and how pensions are linked to earnings
	The existence of minimum floors and/or ceilings
	Maximum amount as % of average earnings
	Duration of contribution/residence period for full pension

b) State pensions (entitlements as dependant)

Access	Married or widowed status required for eligibility
	Provision for pension splitting on divorce
Amount	Whether dependant's entitlement equals that of contributing spouse
	% allocated to wife, if unequal entitlement
	% 'inherited' by widow
	Arrangements for divorcees

c) Private pensions

Access	Balance of state and private pension provision
	Private pensions mandatory or not
	Earnings or duration of service threshold for eligibility
	Ease of transfer or preservation
Amount	Defined contribution or defined benefit
	Level of employer's mandatory contribution, if any
	Whether entitlement is inflation-proofed during preservation
	Whether pension in payment is inflation-proofed
	Level of tax relief on contributions, if any
	Widow's pension as % of deceased member's pension

Source: Ginn et al (2001, chapter 1)

universal, generally reduce the pension for those without a long period of residence.

State pensions derived from a spouse's contribution record vary in the years of marriage required for entitlement, in the proportion that a spouse is entitled to and in the pension rights of divorced spouses (Table 6.2b). Private pensions vary in terms of the extent to which part-timers and the low paid are excluded from access, in arrangements for preserving and transferring entitlements for those who have gaps in employment and job changes, in the level of the contribution required from the employer and whether the pension is a defined amount (Table 6.2c). An important issue for women is the share of state and private pension provision, since state pensions are potentially more adaptable to carers' needs.

Whereas private pensions provide only derived benefits to help carers, most state pensions in the EU have included adaptations that provide some protection for carers' own pensions (see Table 6.3 and Leitner, 2001). This development is most welcome, marking progress towards the independence model of pension provision, in which women (and carers generally) are assisted in building an adequate pension of their own, rather than relying on derived pensions. Later in this chapter, the role of derived pensions is considered more fully.

Among countries with a flat-rate state pension, Britain and Ireland allow those with periods of caring to accrue entitlements during that period (Table 6.3a), but carer protection has only applied since 2002 in the British second tier pension. The Netherlands and Denmark ensure that those who have spent years providing care receive the same basic pension as those who have been continuously employed, by paying a tax-funded 'citizen's pension' to all those fulfilling residence requirements. These universal pensions are payable to men and women in the Netherlands at age 65 and in Denmark at 67, while state pensions are payable in Ireland at 66 (65 if retired) and at 60 for women and 65 for men in Britain (rising to 65 for women by 2020).

Unfortunately, neither carer protection nor a citizen's pension is effective in preventing poverty if the level of the pension is very low, as in Britain. The British basic pension compares very unfavourably with other flat-rate pensions. For example, in 1998 Ireland's basic pension for a lone pensioner was 29% of average industrial earnings (equivalent to £91 per week, compared with Britain's £67), and it is being increased faster than prices (Daly, 2001). In the Netherlands the basic pension for a lone pensioner in 2002 was 203 Euros (about £130) per week plus a holiday allowance, and the pension is indexed to the minimum wage. For an example outside the EU, New Zealanders receive a tax-funded citizen's pension at age 65 set at 34% of average net earnings for each married person and 44% for lone pensioners. In 1998 this was equivalent to over £100 per week for a lone pensioner (using purchasing power parities). As a result, in New Zealand men's and women's incomes in retirement are roughly equal (St John and Gran, 2001). One reason New Zealand has the resources to provide this citizen's pension is that there is no tax relief on private pensions, in contrast to Britain.

Table 6.3: Allowances for childcare or eldercare in state pension schemes (EU15)

a) Flat-rate schemes

Britain (UK)	Home Responsibilities Protection in basic pension for those with children up to 16 (or 18 in full-time education) and for those providing substantial care for adults
Ireland (IRE)	Homemakers Scheme, as above
Denmark (DK)	Pension for all residents, tax-funded
Netherlands (NL)	Pension for all residents, tax-funded

b) Earnings-related schemes

Finland (FI)	Coverage for recipients of home care allowance
Sweden (S)	Four years coverage for each child
Austria (A)	Four years coverage for each child
Germany (D)	Three years coverage for each child; informal carers covered, benefit depending on hours of care provided
France (F)	Two years coverage for each child; bonus for mothers of three children
Belgium (BE)	Two years coverage for each child, based on individual's last wage
Portugal (P)	Two years coverage for each child
Luxembourg (L)	Two years coverage for each child
Spain (E)	One year coverage for each child
Italy (I)	Six months coverage for each child; one month/year coverage for informal carers
Greece (EL)	Three to six months coverage for each child
Denmark: ATP scheme	None, but pension related to hours not earnings
Britain: SERPS/S2P schemes	None in SERPS, but its replacement – the State Second Pension – includes coverage until the youngest child is aged 6

Source: Adapted from Leitner (2001, tables 4 and 5)

Turning to earnings-related state pensions, the 11 EU countries without a basic flat-rate pension all provide some allowance for pension accrual by those with family caring commitments although they vary in generosity (Table 6.3b). In earnings-related schemes, the value of a pension credit depends on the notional contribution rate applied for the period covered, which may be a fraction of national average earnings or of the individual's recent earnings. The British S2P provides carer credits based on notional earnings of about £10,000 pa. Some pension disadvantage due to raising children is likely to remain for those returning to employment after their 'carer coverage' (years when caring allowances apply) runs out, if continuing childcare responsibilities prevent them from obtaining full-time employment in a similar job to their previous one. Another relevant factor is the number of years used in calculating the average earnings on which the pension entitlement is based (Leitner, 2001). Half of the EU countries which have an earnings-related scheme use lifetime earnings

(Belgium, Germany, Italy, Luxembourg, Sweden, Britain); in these countries periods of no/low pay will tend to reduce the average earnings on which the pension is based, unless those periods are entirely covered by pension credits. The remainder use average earnings during the last year or last few years (Finland, Greece, Spain) or the average in the best years (Austria, France, Portugal). Since women's earnings are not necessarily highest towards the end of their working life (as is often the case for men, especially in non-manual occupations), use of best years is more helpful to women than use of last years.

Income replacement rates for those with a typically feminine lifecourse are a useful way of comparing the carer-friendliness of state pensions. Replacement rates at retirement are shown in Table 6.4, for non-married pensioners in five EU countries in the early 1990s (Eurostat, 1993). Those with a short employment history and former wages two thirds of average had net replacement rates ranging from 82% in Denmark to less than a third in Germany and Britain (see Table 6.4, column 4, shaded). In contrast, those with average wages and a full employment record had replacement rates of 60% in Denmark, 77% in Germany and 44% in Britain (Table 6.4, column 2). In terms of replacement rate, the state pension disadvantage due to a typically feminine lifecourse was most severe in Germany and Spain, followed by Britain, while redistribution towards those with such a lifecourse was strongest in Denmark and the Netherlands. Thus state pensions vary across countries in terms of both overall generosity and the extent to which those with family caring responsibilities are disadvantaged. However, all state pensions are more carer-friendly than private pensions.

Private pensions, despite subsidies from public funds through tax relief in most countries, include no provision for periods of caring. Hence, although they formally treat men and women equally, these pensions indirectly discriminate against women, who are the main providers of unpaid family care. Individuals lacking continuous full-time employment are inevitably placed at a disadvantage. Private pensions are becoming more widespread in the EU, while

Table 6.4: Replacement rates[a] for non-married pensioner by qualification period and former wages

Former wages	Full pension			Partial pension (20 yrs)		
	2/3	100%	200%	2/3	100%	200%
Spain	98	97	97	70	73	71
Germany	72	77	63	32	34	28
Denmark	83	60	37	82	59	36
Netherlands	66	49	27	66	49	27
UK	53	44	30	31	28	23

Notes: [a] Net, at retirement, for those receiving the state retirement pension.
Shaded figures represent likely outcomes for women with interrupted employment.

Source: Eurostat (1993)

social insurance schemes are being cut back, modestly in some countries, severely in others such as Britain (Clasen, 1997). The question of enabling preservation and transfer of occupational pension rights across EU borders for mobile workers was being addressed by an EC consultation in 2003, although the different tax regimes in EU member states present formidable obstacles.

The unequal benefits from private pensions according to gender and class have been shown in earlier chapters and in Ginn and Arber (1991, 1999). Therefore a pension system in which state pensions play the major role is essential if progress is to be made towards an independence model of pensions.

Towards an independence model of pensions

Across Europe family structures are changing, with declining marriage rates and rising rates of cohabitation, divorce, lone motherhood and births outside marriage (Dykstra, 2003). The trend towards women raising children independently of a partner, which can be seen as indicating greater autonomy of women as they are freed from traditional family bonds, is strongest in the Nordic welfare states (Denmark, Sweden, Norway and Finland), France and Britain, but is relatively weak in the familialistic Mediterranean countries (Esping-Andersen, 1996).

The rises in divorce, lone parenthood and cohabitation, although less striking in the EU as a whole than in Britain, are unlikely to be reversed, and the decline of marriage as a lifelong contract makes reliance on a husband for an income in later life an ever more risky strategy for women. The unravelling of the ties between marriage and motherhood makes a reassessment of derived benefits urgent. As argued in Chapter Four, survivor benefits are no longer an effective means, if they ever were, of compensating carers for their pension losses. Such benefits serve mainly as a subsidy to marriage, financed by carers and non-carers alike, even though many married couples are childless. Thus the rationale for providing subsidies to non-contributors purely on the basis of their marital status is becoming increasingly dubious. Risk-pooling and redistribution are important and valuable functions of social insurance. Yet pension scheme subsidies flowing from non-married mothers to childless married women raise questions of both equity and efficiency. In a context of serial partnerships across the lifecourse, administering derived benefits is becoming increasingly complex and inefficient for both state agencies and private pension operators. Depending on derived benefits is increasingly fraught with risk for women in the EU (Jepsen and Meulders, 2002). Yet derived benefits cannot be abolished, or even phased out, until suitable alternative means are in place so that those with a typically feminine lifecourse are able to build adequate pensions of their own.

The European Commission, through its Social Protection Committee, urges member states to ensure equal treatment of men and women in pensions legislation, including applying equal actuarial factors to pensions (EC, 2002). Recognising women's pension disadvantages due to their family roles, they also advocate pension credits for childrearing and splitting of pension rights between spouses. However, the EC has not yet explicitly endorsed the independence model of pensions – often referred to as the individualisation of social security rights – as a desirable objective. Doing so would risk opposition from several member states. Yet such a lead from the EC would support the campaigns by pensioners and women's organisations to improve women's prospects of an adequate independent income in later life.

Conclusions

Comparison of EU countries shows that social and employment policies, exemplified in the Nordic welfare states, can do much to help reconcile women's dual roles in reproducing society and in paid employment. If a trade-off between women's social reproduction and economic production can be avoided, or at least minimised, the affordability of state pension schemes is improved by their social insurance contributions and taxes.

Women's chance of an adequate income of their own in retirement depends on both the overall generosity of their country's state pension schemes and the extent to which schemes are carer-friendly – fitted to the needs of those with caring commitments. Among EU countries, Britain has relatively high poverty rates and gender inequality, while the Netherlands stands out as having low poverty rates that are equal for men and women and high pensioner incomes compared with the population as a whole. Significantly, both these countries have well-developed occupational pensions, but the more favourable outcome in the Netherlands may be attributed to its relatively generous universal pension.

Trends in parenting and partnering across the EU point to the need for an independence model of pensions, in which women can receive an adequate income in later life irrespective of their marital status. Yet progress towards phasing out derived pension benefits depends on improving state pensions in terms of their carer-friendliness. In Chapter Seven, I turn to pensions policy, particularly the question of how the tangled British pension system could be better adapted to women's working lives.

SEVEN

British pension policy: a gender perspective on alternative rescue plans

Few outside government deny that the British pension system is now in crisis, although the exact nature of that crisis is variously defined and gender issues are rarely considered. Critical assessments of current policy abound in the evidence submitted to the Work and Pensions Select Committee's inquiry (Work and Pensions Committee, 2002), from pension providers and advisers (over 25 submissions), trades unions including the TUC (10), employer organisations including the Confederation of British Industry (2), pensioner organisations including the National Pensioners Convention (7), major pensioner charities (2), think tanks (4), consumer groups, academics and other individuals.

In this chapter the concerns expressed by a range of such commentators are outlined. The reasons why reaching a pensions consensus has proved so difficult are discussed and the main types of rescue plan proposed are considered, focusing on the gender implications of each. Concerns can be grouped into three main areas – pensioner poverty, erosion of saving incentives and the crisis of private pensions.

Pensioner poverty

Member countries of the EU have agreed that pensions should be adequate to ensure that older people can enjoy a "decent standard of living" (EC, 2002, p 5) but the British government has not said what income this would require. Many experts believe that neither the basic state pension nor the means-tested Minimum Income Guarantee (MIG) is adequate, and that the levels of pensioner poverty in Britain, especially among women, are unacceptable (see Chapter Six).

Cuts in state pensions are set to continue, so that wage replacement rates will decline even further in future and the pensions poverty trap will widen. The government's answer is to expand the system of means-tested benefits through a Pension Credit from October 2003. This will introduce a taper into means testing so that 40% of income above the full basic pension is lost instead of 100% as at present, helping those with incomes slightly above the MIG but also drawing over half of pensioners into means-testing in 2003 and an even larger proportion in future. The government claims the Pension Credit will help women but many older women on low incomes will miss out:

- married or cohabiting women whose partner's income disqualifies them from means-tested benefits;
- women whose basic pension is less than the full amount; they will continue to lose 100% of any second pension or other income, due to the pensions poverty trap;
- women aged between 60 and 65, as the Pension Credit cannot be claimed until age 65;
- those who find it too difficult or demeaning to claim means-tested benefits.

As one important recent report on pension policy concludes, "pensioner poverty is still a key problem" (Brooks et al, 2002, p ii). They could have added that it is primarily a women's problem.

Disincentives to saving due to the pensions poverty trap

The policy of uprating the MIG with earnings but the basic pension only with prices means the basic pension will sink to under half the MIG by 2050, and the State Second Pension (S2P) will be insufficient to close the gap. A person on low wages (under £10,800 per annum in 2002) retiring in 2051 with a complete NI contribution record of 49 years (which could include carer credits) would have a combined basic pension and S2P of £94 per week in 2002 terms, £4 per week less than the MIG (Government Actuary's calculations, cited in Hawksworth, 2002). Even those with a small additional income lifting them above the MIG at retirement would soon sink below that level. And very few individuals will have the full 49 years of NI contributions (or credits) required; the Government Actuary suggests that two thirds entitlement to the S2P is more realistic.

The cost to workers of providing for themselves through private pensions is rising. To obtain a private (DC) pension replacing two thirds of final wages, contributions required have been estimated as 24% of earnings, paid continuously from age 25 to 65, with even higher contributions required for a woman (Mercer, 2002). For the low paid, especially women with gaps in employment, the private pension option was never realistic. Now even the moderately paid must wonder if saving through a private pension is worthwhile. For women the situation is more complex than for men, as their earnings typically fluctuate over the lifecourse. This is illustrated by computer simulations of a range of typical women's lifetime patterns of employment and earnings (Falkingham and Rake, 2001). Whether it will be worthwhile for women to invest in a private pension when their earnings rise depends on unknowable factors such as the level of their future earnings, number of years of their future employment and whether a private pension will provide a higher pension than the S2P. This looks doubtful, especially for those within 20 years of retirement, due to the difficulties affecting private pensions as discussed later in this chapter.

The tapered Pension Credit adds a further layer of complication to the pensions poverty trap. While the numbers of pensioners experiencing a marginal tax rate of over 80% will fall, those facing marginal tax rates over 50% will rise (Clark, 2001). As Brooks et al (2002, p ii) point out, "The Pension Credit does not resolve the incentive problems of the MIG: instead it spreads them out over a much larger group."

Failure of private sector pensions

Many pensioners see the pensions crisis in terms of the low level of state pensions but the term 'pensions crisis' generally refers to the fall in expected amounts of private pensions, following catastrophic losses in private pension funds since 1999. The popularity of personal pensions in the 1980s and early 1990s arose partly from over-generous government financial incentives but also from the sales pitch extrapolating from the high growth rate of equities. Despite past stock market crashes and warnings from academic economists such as Atkinson (1994) that personal pensions are akin to a lottery, many believed in the promise of a 'pot of gold' at retirement. Employees belonging to other DC schemes, including occupational money purchase schemes and group personal pension schemes, are also vulnerable to investment risk. Between 1999 and mid-2002, the FTSE 100 fell from a peak near 7,000 to 4,200, a fall of over 10% per annum (Wachman, 2002), forcing radical reductions in private pension forecasts. In 2002, pension funds recorded their worst investment performance since the mid-1970s, with negative returns estimated as −11%, following −9% in 2001 and −1% in 2000 (Gimbel, 2003). By spring 2003, the FTSE 100 had fallen to the same level as in 1995, about half its level in 1999. Pundits predict a long bear market, with equity prices not expected to rise above 1997 levels for some time (Kay, 2002). Declining annuity rates also affect projected pensions from DC schemes, as insurance companies adjust to increasing life expectancy.

The 80% of occupational pension scheme members who belong to a final salary (FS) scheme may have felt themselves not only better provided for, with higher employer contributions, but also more secure, since their pensions were based on a fixed formula. However, these schemes are not immune to the fall in investment returns, especially since many employers took contribution holidays in the 1990s, leaving their schemes vulnerable to any downturn in the stock market. Some employers boosted their contributions in 2002 to compensate but many others have sought to limit their own risk. Thus the pensions industry is rapidly responding to the combined effects of the slump in the stock market and rising life expectancy, organising conferences on 'Shifting from DB schemes: moving to DC and alternative arrangements' and 'Effectively closing and winding up pension schemes'. Many final salary (defined benefit) schemes have switched to DC plans, with reduced employer contributions and projected pensions some 30% lower than in the original scheme. Some have closed their schemes to new members and others have wound up altogether, with tragic consequences for workers whose expected pension has shrunk overnight to a fraction of its previous level. The Association of Consulting Actuaries, from its own survey, summarises the position of occupational final salary schemes (ACA, 2002):

10% winding up procedures started;
14% scheme closed to future accruals (all contributions cease);
39% scheme closed to new entrants (only members may continue contributions);
18% scheme open to new members but closure under consideration;
19% scheme open to new members, no plans to close.

Britain is almost unique among OECD countries in having no system to protect workers' pensions in the event of business failure or premature closure. The lack of legal restraint on companies wishing to cut back their pension schemes was not recognised as a problem while pension benefits were improving. However, the trend since 2001 towards worsening provision has highlighted the need for more protection of employees (IPRG/NPRG, 2002) and prompted demands from trade unions for legislation. The recent problems in occupational pension schemes may have the unintended effect of narrowing the gender gap in later life income in the future, but this will be the result of men's losses more than women's gains.

Labour's pensions policy

A few months before its election in May 1997, the Labour Party issued a pensions pledge: that, over time, people in retirement would have a sufficient income from the state and second pensions to avoid having to claim means-tested benefits (Labour Party, 1997). Yet once in government, Labour continued Conservative policy of the 1990s, stating its aim to reduce the state's share of pension provision from 60 to 40% of the total by 2050 (DSS, 1998). This policy entails a continuing decline in the basic pension, so that most pensioners will be subject to means-testing either at retirement or soon afterwards. It also threatens to widen the gender gap in later life income.

The reforms introduced since 1997 (see Chapter One) have continued the general thrust of previous Conservative policy in seeking to promote private pensions and reduce state pension provision. Far from achieving the stated aim of a long-term settlement, the reforms have instead provoked widespread dissent. The rift between Labour and the trade unions over pension policy reached the headlines at the 2000 Labour Party conference, as unions insisted on debating the issue of earnings-linking the basic pension.

The government has stubbornly resisted the arguments of a number of authoritative reports stressing the urgency of tackling pensioner poverty through raising and earnings-linking the basic pension (for example, Parker, 2000; Social Security Committee, 2000; Brooks et al, 2002), as well as evidence from academics, pensioner organisations and charities. As Brooks et al (2002) argue, "a policy framework which relies heavily on means testing retirement benefits is flawed" (p vi) and the government's aim to help the poorest, while laudable in principle, is not achieved since the policy "falls short of eliminating pensioner poverty and providing an environment whereby people can understand their entitlements, save and be rewarded for doing so" (p vii).

To understand why a stable consensus in British pension policy has proved elusive, it is helpful to consider how competing objectives have been prioritised by the major political parties and interest groups.

The pensions triangle

Widely accepted essentials of any pension system are that it will at least:

1. ensure adequate pension incomes for the poorest;
2. be affordable in the long term;
3. maintain incentives to save among the working population.

Unfortunately, achieving all three objectives in the triangle simultaneously (see Figure 7.1) is extremely difficult, whereas any two of the three are more easily combined. British governments' attempts to grapple with this unwieldy triangle, prioritising objectives according to ideological preference, have resulted in twists and turns of policy over past decades. In addition, each new reform process has to start from the existing system, which limits the options available, politically and administratively – the constraints of path dependency (Pierson, 2001).

Many countries face questions as to the long-term financial sustainability of their pension system, due to a combination of ageing populations and early exit of workers from the labour force, especially where early pensions are payable. This is not the case in Britain, however, where objective 2 is satisfied but inadequacy of state pensions has been a persistent weakness (see Chapter Six). The Conservatives emphasised objectives 2 and 3 at the cost of adequacy of state pensions, perpetuating poverty among pensioners. During the 1980s and 1990s, income inequality among pensioners grew as the Conservative reforms

Figure 7.1:The pensions policy triangle

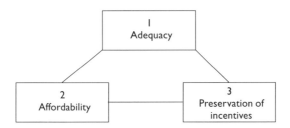

limited spending on state pensions, while tax spending on private pensions accelerated (see Chapter One). The Labour government since 1997 has focused more on the first objective, but mainly through extending means-testing. This has widened the poverty trap, impairing incentives to save and also failing to tackle pensioner poverty effectively. Employers' representatives emphasise the third objective, while also urging increased tax relief for private pensions and a simplification of pension tax regimes (DWP, 2002). Objectives 1 and 3 are prioritised by the pensioner organisations, trade unions, charities and other voluntary organisations, including the Equal Opportunities Commission and the National Assembly of Women (Work and Pensions Committee, 2002). An interesting theoretical alliance has emerged, in that many pension providers and actuaries also advocate boosting the basic pension, because of their interest in objective 3 – incentivising pension saving. It has been argued, but not accepted by government, that objectives 1 and 3 are affordable and would be financially sustainable in the long term given modest increases in NI contributions and full employment.

Labour has carried out no gender audit of the reforms it proposed (and introduced) since 1997. In the next section, some of the main pension proposals made by non-government bodies are considered from a gender perspective.

Alternative pension proposals

Two recent reviews commissioned by the Labour government are concerned with removing barriers to saving through private pensions – the Sandler and Pickering Reviews.

Sandler Report

The chief aim of the inquiry (Sandler, 2002) was to find ways to encourage individuals to save more. The report recommends that a set of safe and simple private savings products, including pension schemes, should be available at low cost, for example through bank branches, supermarkets and on the Internet. This proposal, welcomed by pension providers and insurance companies, seems to ignore the fact that those on low incomes (mainly women) generally cannot afford increased saving and also the danger of mis-selling to those on low incomes.

Pickering Report

This report (Pickering, 2002) is primarily concerned with encouraging the provision of pension schemes by employers through reducing complexity and administrative burdens. Recommendations include simplifying the tax regime under which OPs operate and removing the legal requirements to index-link pensions in payment and provide survivor pensions; allowing employers to make membership of their occupational pension (OP) scheme compulsory for staff if the employer contributes at least 4% of salary; pension rights to take effect immediately upon joining an OP; easier transfer rules; and appointment of a new pensions regulator. Immediate membership of OP schemes and easier pension transfer arrangements could be beneficial to women. Simplification of pension tax treatment is uncontroversial per se. However, insofar as it entails increasing tax relief, this mainly benefits men and reduces public resources available to pay state pensions. The proposal concerning de-indexing has provoked widespread opposition. Its effects would be most severe for women, due to their greater average longevity. Women's groups and trade unions have led the opposition to removal of survivor benefits in OPs, understandably in view of the absence of adequate state pensions to support women in later life. Neither of these controversial proposals to reduce employer costs is likely to be adopted.

Several proposals for reform of state pensions have been made since 2001. Two of these are considered.

Universal Protected Pension (UPP)

Frank Field has proposed introducing a new funded flat-rate compulsory supplement to the basic pension, renaming this hybrid scheme the Universal Protected Pension (UPP) (Deacon, 2002). The UPP would lift pensioner incomes to 25-30% of average earnings, eliminating the need for means-testing. The new supplement would be financed by a 10% increase in workers' National Insurance (NI) contributions. Administration and fund management would be overseen by an independent body of trustees. Existing state second tier pensions, and hence contracting out arrangements, would be ended. The new scheme would cover all individuals as they reached age 25, including all employees and self-employed who pay NI contributions, as well as those who are not employed but who are caring for a child aged up to five and those who are full-time informal carers of other relatives. Field argues that the UPP would have the advantage, compared with simply increasing the basic pension, that the funded part would bring entitlement based on property rights and hence be more attractive to contributors and less subject to the risk of cuts by future governments – political risk. However, the latter claim has been challenged by Willetts (2002), and the existence of the funded element could even increase the temptation for future governments to cut the Pay-As-You-Go element.

From a gender perspective, the UPP offers a similar deal to the basic plus State Second Pension (when the latter becomes a flat-rate scheme in 2007, as planned). The UPP would be similarly redistributive, due to earnings-related NI contributions but flat-rate benefits, and to carer credits. The chief difference is that the combined pension would be substantially higher than under current policy. While this is clearly of benefit to women and the low paid, the 10% increase in NI contributions could equally well be used to improve state pensions in other ways at least as beneficial, as discussed later in this chapter. A major drawback from the point of view of both men and women workers is that the cost of the new funded element of the pension would be borne by the low and moderately paid, as pointed out by Mann (2002). First, a salary ceiling for contributions would limit the contributions paid by high earners (as in the current NI schemes). Second, it is not clear whether employers would be required to pay increased NI contributions for the funded element. If not, the UPP would effectively let employers off the hook, shifting the main burden of financing pensions further towards workers.

Raising and earnings-linking the basic pension

The Institute for Public Policy Research, while sharing the government's aim to direct limited resources to those most in need, has suggested a range of ways to achieve this other than through means testing (Brooks et al, 2002). Their preferred proposal is to raise the basic pension to the level of the Minimum Income Guarantee (£100 per week for a non-married pensioner in 2003) and thereafter index it to national average earnings. The Pension Credit would be scrapped. Variants include making the basic pension universal (a citizen's pension) or using a more generous S2P (instead of raising the basic pension to MIG level) as another way of ensuring individuals can escape means-testing.

IPPR's preferred proposal is estimated to cost 8.6% of GDP by 2050 (Brooks et al, 2002, Table 6.1). Although this is higher than the 6% cost estimated for present policy (including the cost of the Pension Credit), it is still lower than state pension spending projected for any other EU country. Closure of SERPS/S2P and ending rebates for contracting out would reduce the cost of the IPPR proposal to 6.7% of GDP, not substantially more than the cost of current policy, while raising the state pension age to 67 in addition would make the proposal cost-neutral.

Other ways of offsetting the cost of improving the basic pension are considered (Brooks et al, 2002). Some of these increase costs for the better off among the working age population. These include abolishing the Upper Earnings Limit on NI contributions, ending higher rate tax relief on private pensions and phasing out the tax-free lump sum in private pensions. Others, such as freezing the age tax allowance and abolishing the additional tax allowance for married couples aged over 65, would claw back some of the benefit of the improved basic pension from better-off pensioners.

The IPPR's preferred proposal has the great advantage that it would lift most pensioners off means-testing and would radically simplify the state's pension provision so that "people can understand their entitlements, save and be rewarded for doing so" (Brooks et al, 2002, p vii). For women pensioners in particular, the benefits of a higher basic pension would be considerable. However, many older women are not entitled to the full amount, for historical reasons (see Chapter One), leaving them still vulnerable to poverty. In 2000, only 83% of women aged over 60 received any basic pension and the average amount was

71% of the full rate (PPI, 2003). A universal citizen's pension at MIG level, as advocated by the National Association of Pension Funds (NAPF, 2002) would solve this problem. Although Brooks et al (2002) argue that a citizen's pension is unnecessary since by 2020 most women will retire with a full basic pension in their own right, this good news will not help the oldest generation of women. Financing the preferred reform proposal by raising the state pension age has the disadvantage that it would bear hardest on those unable to maintain employment until age 67 due to ill-health, lack of local jobs or informal care responsibilities.

A drawback of IPPR's alternative of abolishing the state second tier pension is that it would leave individuals with no alternative to private pensions, if they wished to build additional pension entitlements. Yet private pensions include no carer-friendly features. There is no good reason to remove the option of the earnings-related SERPS (now named S2P), a fully portable and competitive defined benefit pension that is advantageous for women. Abolishing the state second tier pension would seem "perverse just as the weaknesses of private occupational and individual pensions are becoming increasingly evident" (Catalyst, 2002, p 25).

The general thrust of the IPPR's proposals, if not every detail, chimes with the views of many organisations, including the National Pensioners Convention, TUC, Equal Opportunities Commission, Women's National Commission, Help the Aged, Age Concern, The Work Foundation, Pensions Policy Institute, individual trades unions and local pensioner organisations, as well as representatives of private pension providers (ACA, 2002b; NAPF, 2002). These are united in opposition to the complexity of the current pension system, the inadequacy of state pensions and the extension of means-testing. Despite this critical consensus, there is no sign that the government's view has changed, as discussed in the next section.

Government plans for the future of pensions

The 2002 government Green Paper on pensions (DWP, 2002) is disappointing. There is no new thinking on how to improve the pensions of older people and a complacent tone suggests the government is not concerned at the persistence of poverty levels that are exceptional in Europe, nor at the unpopularity and ineffectiveness of means-testing. While the risks in private pensions and the lesser ability of some population groups, notably women, to acquire an adequate retirement income through these pensions are acknowledged, the policy of privatisation is to continue. The emphasis is on persuading individuals to save more for retirement through private pensions, although no justification for preferring private to state pensions is provided. Moreover, the burden of extra saving is to be borne by workers, not employers, despite the fact that employers' mandatory contributions to social insurance are considerably lower than in most developed economies.

Proposals to encourage the over-fifties back to work are welcome but their effectiveness will depend on ending age discrimination by employers and the availability of suitable attractive jobs. This is especially so in those areas of industrial decline where a particularly high proportion of men aged over 50 are out of work (Catalyst, 2002). The Green Paper also proposes to simplify the pensions tax regime (while increasing tax subsidies for private pensions), to replace the Minimum Funding Requirement (MFR) in occupational pension schemes and to provide a degree of protection against employer fraud or insolvency for workers contributing to employer schemes. However, the removal of the MFR may increase risk for scheme members.

The Green Paper includes a chapter specifically on women, in which the pensions problem arising from the impact of caring roles on full-time employment and earnings is acknowledged, as is their need for pensions independent of a partner. However, this chapter, which has been described as "woeful" (The Work Foundation, 2003, p 7) contains no proposals to help older women other than more means testing. It is also light on proposals to improve pensions for working age women, relying on the redistributive nature of the S2P (despite the well-established inadequacy of the combined basic pension and S2P) and on several welcome reforms to support working-age women's employment. Building on earlier measures to stimulate employment (described and assessed in Millar, 2002), the new measures introduced from April 2003 include the Child Tax Credit and Working Tax Credit. These will make employment more worthwhile for many of those with caring responsibilities but they do little to build pension entitlements, since employee contributions are related to earnings, not tax credits. The level of maternity pay will increase (from £75 to £100 per week) as will its duration (from 18 to 26 weeks), while fathers will be allowed two weeks paternity leave (at £100 per week). There is also a promise of an extra 250,000 childcare places by 2006 (DTI, 2003). Improving pensions information for women is seen as helping them to make better choices, although arguably the chief obstacle to informed choice is the Byzantine nature of the present system. The inequity of lower annuity rates for women is admitted but there are no plans to require equal rates – only the lame advice to 'shop around' for best value. A major weakness of the chapter on women is its lack of solutions for women pensioners' poverty.

Proposals designed to help women build better state pension entitlements are provided by Age Concern/Fawcett Society (2003) in their response to the Green Paper. These include:

• replacing HRP with carer credits;
• relaxing the requirements to qualify for credits when caring for adult dependants;
• reducing the years required to qualify for a full basic pension;
• allowing backdated NI contributions beyond the six years currently allowed.

If reforms on these lines were combined with an increased basic pension, women of all ages would benefit.

The contrast between the government's pension policy and the kind of proposals endorsed widely across civil society could not be more stark, nor more different in terms of gender implications. A common reason advanced by governments for cutting state pensions and instead promoting saving through private pensions is that better state pensions are unaffordable, contravening the objective of sustainability (Figure 7.1). It is worth examining the validity of this argument.

Affordability of better state pensions

Unlike many other developed countries, notably Japan and Italy, Britain does not face a steep rise in the proportion of the older to the working age population in the next 50 years. As a recent analysis points out (Catalyst, 2002), although the number of working-age individuals to each older individual is estimated to fall from about 3.4 in 2000 to a low of 2.4 in 2041 (GAD, 2002), this number has already fallen from 14 in 1900, a steeper rate of fall yet without catastrophic consequences. A more appropriate ratio in assessing the impact of an ageing population on pension scheme viability is the number of pensioners to the number employed. It is estimated that this ratio will be the same in 2030 as in 1999 if two million more people are employed (Catalyst, 2002). About nine million people of working age (or 30% of the working-age population) are not employed, providing ample scope for increasing the numbers employed, especially among those aged over 50 in depressed regions of Britain and among women. Rising productivity also mitigates any adverse effects of an ageing population (Mullan, 2000). "On present trends the worker in 2041 will be the equivalent of more than two workers today" (Catalyst, 2002, p 10). Thus fears of a 'demographic time bomb' and pension unaffordability have been grossly exaggerated in Britain, serving as a pretext for cutting state pension but lacking foundation. Even if the population were ageing rapidly, private funded pensions would be affected just as much as state Pay-As-You-Go pensions (although through different mechanisms), since all pensions are ultimately funded from the wealth created by the working-age population.

Alternative proposals for state pensions such as the IPPR's outlined above (Brooks et al, 2002) have been routinely dismissed by British governments as unaffordable, despite analyses by experts showing that, although net costs would rise, the increases are not unmanageable (see Hancock and Sutherland, 1997; Sutherland, 1998; Brooks et al, 2002). Moreover, phasing out tax relief on private pensions (£13.7 billion in 2000, see Chapter One) would provide savings worth over 40% of the cost of the basic pension. The claim of unaffordability is increasingly unconvincing due to the growing NI surplus arising from earnings-linked contributions and price-linked benefits. A Government Actuary Report (GAD, 2000) estimated that earnings linking would require a rise in combined NI contribution rates from 20% in 2000 to 23% in 2010 and 30% in 2060 (plus 0.75% on all these figures due to basic pension increases in April 2001). But, significantly, the Government Actuary commented that, due to projected real earnings growth, "Even with higher contribution rates real net income [of workers] would still be significantly higher in 2060 than it is now". By March 2002 the NI fund surplus had grown to £24.2 billion, representing 52% of all social security payments and "substantially above the recommended minimum level" of £4 billion (GAD, 2002b, p 10).

The government's intransigence in the face of a consensus among both experts and the public – the principle of collective responsibility for welfare through the National Insurance system is widely supported (Stafford, 1998) – is at first sight puzzling, especially given the Labour Party's historical affinity with the welfare state. However, both Conservative and Labour governments since 1980 have been influenced by neo-liberal ideology, preferring saving through private pensions to collective saving through the National Insurance (NI) schemes. This preference persists despite evidence that private pensions do not necessarily provide better value for money than state pensions; indeed the reverse may be the case as the risks associated with investment clearly show. Glennerster (1999, p 10) asks: "Given these risks, why is the government so keen to see a continuing shift to private pensions?"

The answers usually offered – an ageing population, economic benefits of increased pension funds and the political risk in state pensions – have been challenged. Economists have exploded the myth that an ageing population presents a greater threat to the sustainability of state pensions, because of their Pay-As-You-Go funding, than to private pensions funded by investment of contributions. As Downs (2003) argues, both types of pension must ultimately be paid from the wealth produced by the working-age population and both are at risk if that wealth creation falters due to a decline in the numbers employed or in their productivity. The question of whether high levels of pension saving bring economic benefits is controversial, with no consensus among economists as to whether increased pension saving merely causes a switch from other forms of investment, nor as to whether higher net levels of savings are beneficial (Mabbett, 1997). The example of Japan, with high savings but a stagnant economy, suggests other factors are more important for economic growth. State pensions are indeed subject to political risk but to argue for a reduced role on these grounds is to engage in a self-fulfilling prophecy (Hills, 1995; Downs, 2003). A more constructive approach to the risk of cuts in state pensions might be to seek cross-party agreement to respect properly costed state pension promises. This would act as a brake on the over-frequent reforms that have led to an excessively complex system and eroded public confidence. Whether to provide pensions mainly through social insurance or the private sector is a political choice, with no economic justification for privatisation (Minns, 2001).

Summary and discussion

Earlier chapters have shown the gender implications of British pension policy, in which the interrelation of state, family and market lead to severe pension penalties for most women. In the context of meagre and declining state pensions in Britain, those unable to build a good private pension are at risk of personal poverty in later life, dependent for financial support on family members or on means-tested benefits.

Childcare commitments restrict the full-time employment of mothers, reducing their earnings and accumulation of private pension entitlements. The private pension disadvantage is especially acute for those who bring up children on their own, although once their children are older, divorced and separated women show greater attachment to the labour market than married mothers. Motherhood reduces full-time employment, earnings and private pension coverage for women at all levels of educational qualifications, although the effect is least for the fifth of women who are graduates and greatest for the third of women with mid-level qualifications. Since private pension coverage is strongly related to occupational class, which depends on educational level and work experience, mothers tend to be differentiated in terms of their pension prospects. Only an elite minority, comprising highly qualified partnered mothers and childless women, are likely to obtain private pensions comparable with the average amount for men. Ethnicity interacts with gender, so that the adverse effects of being female on private pension coverage are more severe among the major Asian ethnic groups than among black or white people.

Although a minority of British women – those able to pursue a typically masculine lifecourse, in terms of continuous full-time employment and rising earnings – may be able to obtain a better income in later life than their mothers, most women will be unlikely to do so. The pension future may be bleak for men as well. A decline in men's full-time employment suggests that men's pensions may become less adequate in the future. Much depends on policies to improve employment opportunities for all and on the direction of future pension policies.

The decline in lifelong marriage makes it increasingly important for women to have their own independent pensions. The loosening link between marriage and motherhood, together with women's greater participation in employment and changing attitudes to financial dependence, makes derived benefits increasingly anachronistic. Cross-subsidies in state and private pension schemes in favour of married women may be less appropriate than in the past, although phasing out derived benefits without a positive move towards an independence model of pensions would leave women and other carers worse off. The experience of countries that have abolished derived benefits in state pensions, such as a citizen's pension set at a decent level as in the Netherlands, shows that other ways can be found to ensure women with caring commitments can obtain an adequate independent income in later life.

British social policies increasingly reflect an assumption that both men and women are able to engage in paid work throughout the lifecourse – the demise of the male breadwinner model in policy thinking. In the past, this model had the advantage of supporting married women in their caring roles but the disadvantage of reducing their capacity to protect themselves financially. Moving towards an independence model, in which women's financial security is based on their own labour market contribution, releases resources for the economy and for women themselves. But as Pascall and Lewis argue, this model is only viable if there is a "clearer political acceptance of care as work which has to be properly valued" (2000, p 17). According to McDonald (2000), the collapse of birth rates in most developed societies shows the failure of a market-driven approach to policy. He advocates a new social contract in which just rewards are provided for social reproduction – "Society must attempt to equalise the economic outcomes for different family configurations" – recognising that "children are a social good and not merely a private optional pleasure" (McDonald, 2000). This requires that family caring is acknowledged as work and treated accordingly by provision of adequate supportive care services; that there is more equal sharing of paid and unpaid work between partners, with incentives to provide care and measures to end the scandalously long hours worked by British men; and that there is compensation for carers' loss of earnings and pension entitlements. Esping-Andersen (2002) shows that family-friendly social and employment policies in Nordic countries promote both women's employment and fertility, concluding that a "rewritten gender contract" (p 66) is required to enable women to succeed in combining paid work and childrearing.

Conclusions

The book has examined how the gendered lifecourse can lead to pension inequalities, especially where effective policies to support those with caring responsibilities through state services are lacking and where private (occupational and personal) pensions play a major role. Britain's pension system is an outlier internationally in the emphasis placed on private pensions at the expense of state pensions. Even among countries with a well-developed private pension sector, Britain is the only country where private pensions are designed as alternatives to the state second tier pension rather than as a means of additional saving on top of state pensions. These peculiarities explain both the relatively low level of most British pensioners' incomes and the pension disadvantage of older women compared with other EU countries where social insurance is still accepted as the chief means of providing retirement income (Clasen, 1997).

While state pensions are being run down, private pensions are in no shape to take on even part of their role. The policy of promoting private pensions at the expense of state pensions is in urgent need of review, not least because it fails to tackle the serious gender inequalities in pension prospects. No convincing case has been made for the advantages of the private sector in terms of delivering pensions. The Pensions Policy Institute predict that spending only 5% of GDP on state pensions but half as much again on private pension tax reliefs will increase inequality among pensioners, concluding that debate on the distributive implications of the state–private pensions mix is urgent (PPI, 2003). British governments, in attributing people's reluctance to save more through the private sector to irrationality or ignorance, show a failure to appreciate the often sound reasons they have. An inherent weakness of private pensions is the high level of risk involved for contributors, especially the less well-off. Moreover, private pensions allow the costs of caring to lie where they fall, mainly on women in later life: the market cannot fulfil the social function of protecting the pensions of those who raise the next generation.

State pension schemes, in contrast, have the potential to ensure that the pension costs of family caring are fairly shared between those who undertake such tasks and those who do not. A radical reform to achieve this aim would replace the basic state pension with a citizen's pension set at a level high enough to prevent poverty and indexed to national standards of living. This would allow all individuals the dignity and security of their own income in later life and improve gender equality in retirement incomes. It would be easy to understand and would preserve incentives for further savings through private pensions or other means. A less drastic reform would substantially raise and earnings-link the basic pension, while revitalising the State Earnings Related Pension Scheme, including either carer credits or a 'best years' formula. Such reforms are affordable in a rich country, yet retirement for the majority of today's young women is likely to be blighted by personal poverty unless the direction of pension policy changes.

If "reproduction – the renewal and development of the next generation in the family – is seen as worthy of public appreciation and support" (Joshi, 2000, p 22), it is time that policy makers designed pensions to fit the gendered nature of the lifecourse.

References

ACA (Association of Consulting Actuaries) (2002a) *ACA survey of final salary schemes*, www.aca.org.uk/public_content/June_2002_ACA_SURVEY_OF_FINAL_SALARY_SCHEMES.doc.

ACA (2002b) 'Memorandum (PEN36)', in *The future of UK pensions*, Vol III, HC 92-III, London: The Stationery Office.

Adema, W. (2000) 'Revisiting real social spending across countries: a brief note', *OECD Economic Studies*, vol 30, pp 191-7.

Age Concern/Fawcett Society (2003) *Simplicity, security and choice: A joint response on women and pensions*, London: Age Concern/Fawcett Society.

Agulnik, P. and Le Grand, J. (1998) 'Tax relief and partnership pensions', *Fiscal Studies*, vol 19, no 4, pp 403-28.

Aldridge, A. (1998) '*Habitus* and cultural capital in the filed of personal finance', *The Sociological Review*, vol 46. no 1, pp 1-23.

Allatt, P. (1981) 'Stereotyping: familism in the law', chapter 8 in B. Fryer, A. Hunt, D. Mcbarnet and B. Moorhouse (eds) *Law, state and society*, London: Croom Helm.

Arber, S. (1989) 'Class and the elderly', *Social Studies Review*, vol 4, no 3, pp 90-5.

Arber, S. and Ginn, J. (1991) *Gender and later life: A sociological analysis of resources and constraints*, London: Sage Publications.

Arber, S. and Ginn, J. (1995) 'The mirage of gender equality: occupational success in the labour market and within marriage', *British Journal of Sociology*, vol 46, no 1, pp 21-43.

Atkinson, A. (1994) *State pensions for today and tomorrow*, London: London School of Economics and Political Science/Suntory Toyota International Centre of Economics and Related Disciplines.

Bagavos, C. and Martin, C. (eds) (2000) 'Low fertility, families and public policies', Synthesis Report on Annual Seminar held in Seville, 15-16 September, Vienna: Austrian Institute for Family Studies/European Observatory on Family Matters.

Baldwin, S. and Falkingham, J. (eds) (1994) *Social security and social change: New challenges to the Beveridge Model*, Hemel Hempstead: Harvester Wheatsheaf.

Banks, J., Blundell, R., Disney, R. and Emmerson, C. (2002) *Retirement, pensions and the adequacy of saving: A guide to the debate*, Briefing Note no 29, London: Institute for Fiscal Studies.

Barber v GRE Assurance Group [1990] Case No C-262-88, ECR-I-1889.

Bardasi, E. and Jenkins, S. (2002) *Income in later life: Work history matters*, Bristol/York: The Policy Press/Joseph Rowntree Foundation.

Beets, G. (1999) 'Education and age at first birth', *Demos*, vol 15, no 8, Special Issue on European Population Conference 1999, also www.nidi.nl/public/demos/dm99epc2.html.

Berthoud, R. (1998) *The incomes of ethnic minorities*, Colchester: Institute for Social and Economic Research.

Beveridge, W. (1942) *Social insurance and allied services*, Cmnd 6404, London: HMSO.

Blackburn, R. (2002) *Banking on death or investing in life*, London: Verso.

Blossfeld, H.-P. and Hakim, C. (eds) (1997) *Between equalisation and marginalisation: Women working part time in Europe and the United States*, Oxford: Oxford University Press.

Bradshaw, J., Kennedy, S., Kilkey, M., Hutton, S., Corden, A., Eardley, T., Holmes, H. and Neale, J. (1996) *The employment of lone parents: A comparison of policy in 20 countries*, London: Family Policy Studies Centre.

Brannen, J. (1999) 'Caring for children', in S. Walby (ed) *New agendas for women*, Basingstoke: Macmillan.

Brooks, R., Regan, S. and Robinson, P. (2002) *A new contract for retirement*, London: Institute for Public Policy Research.

Buck, N. and Ermisch, J. (1995) 'Cohabitation in Britain', in *Changing Britain*, October, Newsletter of the Population and Household Change Research Programme, Colchester: Essex University.

Burton, D. (1997) 'Ethnicity and occupational welfare: a study of pension scheme membership', *Work, Employment and Society*, vol 11, no 3, pp 505-18.

Catalyst (2002) *The challenge of longer life. Economic burden or social opportunity?*, London: Catalyst.

CBI (Confederation of British Industry) (1985) *CBI response to the Green Paper on Reform of Social Security*, London: CBI.

CEC (Commission of the European Communities) (2003) *Joint Report by the Commission and the Council on Adequate and Sustainable Pensions*, Brussels: CEC.

Chevalier, A. and Viitanen, T. (2002) *The supply of childcare in Britain: Do mothers queue for childcare?*, Mimeo, Institute for the Study of Social Change, Dublin: University College.

Clark, T. (2001) *Recent pensions policy and the pensions credit*, Briefing Note no 17, London: Institute for Fiscal Studies.

Clasen, J. (ed) (1997) *Social insurance in Europe*, Bristol: The Policy Press.

Cloud, K. and Garrett, N. (1996) 'A modest proposal for the inclusion of women's household production in analysis of structural transformation', *Feminist Economics*, vol 2, no 3, pp 93-120.

Coleman, D. (2000) 'Trends and regional variations in European fertility', in C. Bagavos and C. Martin (eds) 'Low fertility, families and public policies', Synthesis Report on Annual Seminar held in Seville, September 15-16, Vienna: Austrian Institute for Family Studies/European Observatory on Family Matters.

Cooper, H., Arber, S., Smaje, C. and Ginn, J. (1999) *Ethnic differences in the health and health related behaviour of older people*, London: HEA.

Corden, A. (1999) 'Claiming entitlement: take-up of benefits', in J. Ditch (ed) *Introduction to social security*, London: Routledge.

Cousins, C. (1994) 'A comparison of the labour market position of women in Spain and the United Kingdom with reference to the flexible labour debate', *Work, Employment and Society*, vol 8, no 1, pp 45-67.

CPAG (Child Poverty Action Group) (1998) *Real choices for lone parents and their children*, London: CPAG.

Crompton, R. and Harris, F. (1999) 'Attitudes, women's employment, and the changing domestic division of labour: a cross national analysis', in R. Crompton (ed) *Restructuring gender relations and employment*, Oxford: Oxford University Press.

Cuvillier, R. (1979) 'The housewife: an unjustifiable burden on the community', *Journal of Social Policy*, vol 8, no 1, pp 1-26.

Dale, A. and Holdsworth, C. (1998) 'Why don't minority ethnic women in Britain work part time?', in J. O'Reilly and C. Fagan (eds) *Part-time prospects*, London: Routledge.

Daly, M. (1996) *Social security, gender and equality in the European Union*, Brussels: EC DGV.

Daly, M. (2001) 'Between means-testing and social insurance: women's pensions in Ireland', in J. Ginn, D. Street and S. Arber (eds) *Women, work and pensions: International issues and prospects*, Buckingham: Open University Press.

Davies, B. and Ward, S. (1992) *Women and personal pensions*, London: Equal Opportunities Commission.

Davies, H., Joshi, H. and Peronaci, R. (2000) 'Forgone income and motherhood: what do recent British data tell us?', *Population Studies*, vol 54, pp 293-305.

Daycare Trust (1999) *Childcare gaps*, London: Daycare Trust.

Daycare Trust (2000) *No more nine to five: Childcare in a changing world*, London: Daycare Trust.

Daycare Trust (2001) *The price parents pay. Sharing the costs of childcare*, London: Daycare Trust.

Daycare Trust (2002) *Childcare costs survey 2002*, London: Daycare Trust.

Deacon, A. (ed) (2002) *Debating pensions. Self interest, citizenship and the common good*, London: Civitas.

Dex, S. (1987) *Women's occupational mobility: A lifetime perspective*, Basingstoke: Macmillan.

Dex, S., Joshi, H. and Macran, S. (1996) 'A widening gulf among British mothers', *Oxford Review of Economic Policy*, vol 12, no 1, pp 65-75.

Dilnot, A., Disney, R., Johnson, P. and Whitehouse, E. (1994) *Pensions policy in the UK. An economic analysis*, London: Institute of Fiscal Studies.

Disney, R. and Johnson, P. (1997) 'The UK: a working system of minimum pensions?', Paper presented to conference on Redesigning Social Security, Kiel Institute of World Economics, Kiel, 26-27 June.

Dooghe, G. and Appleton, N. (1995) *Elderly women in Europe. Choices and challenges*, London: Anchor Housing.

Downs, C. (2003) 'Pay as you go funding for pensions: panacea or pariah?', *Citizen's Income Newsletter*, vol 1: 1-10.

DSS (Department of Social Security) (1994) *Personal pension statistics 1992/3*, revised edition, London: Government Statistical Service.

DSS (1996) *Family Resources Survey: Great Britain 1994/5*, London: HMSO.

DSS (1998) *A new contract for welfare: Partnership in pensions*, Cm 4179, London: The Stationery Office.

DSS (1999) *The structure of rebates for the second state pension*, London: DSS.

DSS (2000) *Households Below Average Income*, London: DSS.

DTI (Department of Trade and Industry) (2003) *Balancing work and family life: Enhancing choice and support for parents*, London: HM Treasury.

Duncan, S. (2002) 'Policy discourses on "reconciling work and life" in the EU', *Social Policy and Society*, vol 1, no 4, pp 305-14.

Durham, P. (1994) 'Millions will lose money on private pensions', *Independent*, 28 March.

DWP (Department of Work and Pensions) (2002) *Simplicity, security and choice: Working and saving for retirement*, Cm 5677, London: The Stationery Office.

Dykstra, P. (2003) 'Changes in family patterns and people's lives: Western European trends', in T. Knijn and A. Komter (eds) *Solidarity between the sexes and the generations*, Aldershot: Edward Elgar.

EC (European Commission) (2002) 'Broad common objectives and working methods in the area of pensions', Part II of *Joint Report of the Social Protection Committee and the Economic Policy Committee*, Brussels: EC.

EPC (Economic Policy Committee) (2001) *Budgetary challenges posed by an ageing population*, Brussels: EPC of the EC, and at http://europa.eu.int/comm/economy_finance/epc.en.htm.

Esping-Andersen, G. (1996) 'Welfare states without work: the impasse of labour shedding and familialism in continental European social policy', in G. Esping-Andersen (ed) *Welfare states in transition*, London: Sage Publications.

Esping-Andersen, G. (1999) 'The household economy', in G. Esping-Andersen, *Social foundations of postindustrial economies*, Oxford: Oxford University Press.

Esping-Andersen, G. (2002) *Why we need a new welfare state*, Oxford: Oxford University Press.

Esping-Andersen, G. (2002) 'A new gender contract', in G. Esping-Andersen (ed) *Why we need a new welfare state,* Oxford: Oxford University Press, ch 3.

Eurostat (1993) *Old age replacement ratios, Vol 1: Relation between pensions and income from employment at the moment of retirement*, Luxembourg: Statistical Office.

Eurostat (2001) *The social situation in the European Union 2001*, Luxembourg: Office for the Official Publication of the European Communities.

Eurostat (2002) *The social situation in the European Union 2002*, Luxembourg: Office for the Official Publication of the European Communities.

Evason, E. and Spence, L. (2002) *Women and pensions*, Belfast: Equality Commission for Northern Ireland.

Evason, E., Dowds, L. and Devine, P. (2002) 'Pensioners and the Minimum Income Guarantee: observations from recent research', *Journal of Social Policy and Administration*, vol 36, no 1, pp 36-45.

Eversheds Pensions Law Team (2000) *Pensions law handbook 2001*, London: Eversheds.

Falkingham, J. and Rake, K. (2001) 'Modelling the gender impact of British pension reforms', in J. Ginn, D. Street and S. Arber (eds) *Women, work and pensions*, Buckingham: Open University Press, pp 67-85.

Falkingham, J., Rake, K. and Paxton, W. (2002) *Modelling pension choices for the 21st century*, London: Sage Publications.

Family Resources Surveys (1994, 1995, 1996) Computer files held at the Data Archive, Essex University.

Fast, J., Eales, J. and Keating, N. (2001) *Economic impact of health, income security and labour policies on informal caregivers of frail seniors*, Ottawa, ON: Status of Women Canada and www.swc-cfc.gc.ca/publish/research/010514-0662654765-e.html#TOP

Fast, J., Williamson, D. and Keating, N. (1999) 'The hidden costs of informal elder care', *Journal of Family and Economic Issues*, vol 20, no 3, pp 301-26.

Field, J. (2000) *Pensions and divorce: The 1998 survey, Department of Social Security Research Report no 117*, London: Corporate Document Services.

Field, J. and Farrant, G. (1993) 'Public perceptions of occupational schemes', in R. Goode (ed) *Pension law reform: The report of the Pension Law Reform Committee. Vol 2, The Research*, London: HMSO.

FPSC (Family Policy Studies Centre) (1998) *Families and childcare*, Family Briefing Paper no 6, London: FPSC.

FPSC (1999) *Family finances and property on divorce: A guide to the issues*, Family Briefing Paper no 10, London: FPSC.

FPSC (2000) 'New options and new ways of living', *Families Today*, Factsheet no 1, pp 3-4.

GAD (Government Actuary Department) (2000) *Report by the Government Actuary on the cost of uprating the basic retirement pension in line with the general level of earnings*, Cm 4920, London: The Stationery Office.

GAD (2002a) *National Population Projections, 2000-based*, London: The Stationery Office.

GAD (2002b) *Report by the Government Actuary on the drafts of the Social Security Benefits Uprating Order 2002 and the Social Security (Contributions) (Re-rating and National Insurance Funds Payments) Order 2002*, London: The Stationery Office (also at www.gad.gov.uk/publications/docs/2002uprating.pdf).

GHS (General Household Survey) data (1993/94, 1994/95, 1995/96 and 1996/97), Computer files held at the Data Archive, University of Essex, Colchester.

Gershuny, J. (1997) 'Sexual divisions and the distribution of work in the household', chapter 13 in G. Dench (ed) *Rewriting the sexual contract*, London: Institute of Community Studies.

Gershuny, J., Godwin, M. and Jones, S. (1994) 'The domestic labour revolution: a process of lagged adaptation?', in M. Anderson, F. Bechofer and J. Gershuny (eds) *The social and political economy of the household*, Oxford: Oxford University Press.

Gimbel, F. (2003) 'Trustee pay storm in UK top 50', *Financial Times Fund Management*, page 1, www.ft.com/ftfm.

Ginn, J. and Arber, S. (1991) 'Gender, class and income inequalities in later life', *British Journal of Sociology*, vol 42, no 3, pp 369-96.

Ginn, J. and Arber, S. (1992) 'Towards women's independence: pension systems in three contrasting European welfare states', *Journal of European Social Policy*, vol 2, no 4, pp 255-77.

Ginn, J. and Arber, S. (1993) 'Pension penalties: the gendered division of occupational welfare', *Work, Employment and Society*, vol 7, no 1, pp 47-70.

Ginn, J. and Arber, S. (1996) 'Patterns of employment, pensions and gender: the effect of work history on older women's non-state pensions', *Work, Employment and Society*, vol 10, no 3, pp 469-90.

Ginn, J. and Arber, S. (1998) 'How does part-time work lead to low pension income?', in J. O'Reilly and C. Fagan (eds) *Part-time prospects*, London: Routledge.

Ginn, J. and Arber, S. (1999) 'Changing patterns of pension inequality: the shift from state to private sources', *Ageing and Society*, vol 19, no 3, pp 319-42.

Ginn, J. and Arber, S. (2000a) 'Personal pension take-up in the 1990s in relation to position in the labour market', *Journal of Social Policy*, vol 29, no 2, pp 205-28.

Ginn, J. and Arber, S. (2000b) 'Ethnic inequality in later life: variation in financial circumstances by gender and ethnic group', *Education and Ageing*, vol 15, no 1, pp 65-83.

Ginn, J. and Arber, S. (2000c) 'Pension costs of caring', *Benefits*, no 28, May/June, pp 13-17.

Ginn, J. and Arber, S. (2001) 'Pension prospects of minority ethnic groups', *British Journal of Sociology*, vol 52, no 3, pp 519-39.

Ginn, J. and Arber, S. (2002) 'Degrees of freedom: can graduate women avoid the motherhood gap in pensions?', *Sociological Research On-line*, www.socresonline.org.uk/7/2/.

Ginn, J. and Price, D. (2002) 'Can divorced women catch up in pension building?', *Child and Family Law Quarterly*, vol 14, no 2, pp 157-73.

Glennerster, H. (1999) 'The elderly: a burden on the economy?', *Centrepiece*, Summer, pp 6-12.

Glover, J. and Arber, S. (1995) 'Polarisation in mothers' employment', *Gender, Work and Organisation*, vol 2, no 4, pp 165-79.

Goode, R. (1993) *Pension law reform: The report of the Pension Law Review Committee*, vols I, II, Cm 2342-1, London: HMSO.

Gornick, J., Meyers, M. and Ross, K. (1997) 'Supporting the employment of mothers: policy variation across fourteen welfare states', *Journal of European Social Policy*, vol 7, no 1, pp 45-70.

Grace, M. (1998) 'The work of caring for young children: priceless or worthless?', *Women's Studies International Forum*, vol 21, no 4, pp 401-13.

Green, F., Hadjimatheou, G. and Smail, R. (1984) *Unequal fringes: Fringe benefits in the United Kingdom*, London: Bedford Square Press/NCVO.

Gregg, P., Knight, G. and Wadsworth, J. (2000) '"Heaven knows I'm miserable now": job insecurity in the British labour market', in E. Heary and J. Salmon (eds) *The insecure workforce*, Routledge: London.

Griffiths, K. (2002) 'Low cost pensions miss female target group in first year', *Independent*, 30 March, www.independent.co.uk/story.jsp?story=279889.

Groves, D. (1987) 'Occupational pension provision and women's poverty in old age', in C. Glendinning and J. Millar (eds) *Women and poverty in Britain*, Brighton: Wheatsheaf, pp 199-217.

Groves, D. (1991) 'Financial provision for women in retirement', in M. Maclean and D. Groves (eds) *Women's issues in social policy*, London: Routledge, pp 141-62.

Hakim, C. (1993) 'The myth of rising female employment', *Work, Employment and Society*, vol 7, pp 97-120.

Hakim, C. (2000) *Work lifestyles choices in the 21st century: preference theory*, Oxford: Oxford University Press.

Hancock, R. and Sutherland, H. (1997) *The costs and distributional effects of increasing the basic state pension*, London: Age Concern.

Hannah, L. (1986) *Inventing retirement: The development of occupational pensions in Britain*, Cambridge: Cambridge University Press.

Harkness, S. (2002) *Low pay, times of work and gender*, Manchester: Equal Opportunties Commission.

Harkness, S. and Waldfogel, J. (1999) *The family gap in pay: Evidence from seven industrialised countries*, CASE paper no 29, London: Centre for Analysis of Social Exclusion.

Haskey, J. (1994) 'Estimated numbers of one parent familiesand their prevalence in Great Britain in 1991', *Population Trends 78*, London: HMSO.

Haskey, J. (1998) 'One-parent families and their dependent children in Great Britain', *Population Trends 91*, Spring, London: The Stationery Office, pp 5-14.

Hawkes, C. and Garman, A. (1995) *Perceptions of non-state pensions*, In-house Report no 8, London: Department of Social Security.

Hawksworth, J. (2002) *A new contract for retirement: Modelling policy options to 2050*, London: PriceWaterhouseCoopers.

Hills, J. (1995) 'The welfare state and redistribution between generations', in J. Falkingham and J. Hills (eds) *The dynamic of welfare. Social policy and the life cycle*, Hemel Hempstead: Harvester Wheatsheaf.

Himmelweit, S. (1998) 'Accounting for caring', *Radical Statistics*, no 70, Winter, pp 1-8.

Hochschild, A. (1989) *The second shift: Working parents and the revolution at home*, New York, NY: Viking.

Holdsworth, C. and Dale, A. (1997) 'Ethnic differences in women's employment', *Work, Employment and Society*, vol 11, no 3, pp 435-57.

House of Commons (2002) Government answer to Parliamentary Question from Webb, 21 June, derived from the Pensioners' Income Series.

Hutton, S., Kennedy, S. and Whiteford, P. (1995) *Equalization of state pension ages: The gender impact*, Manchester: Equal Opportunities Commission.

IPRG (Independent Pensions Research Group)/NPRG (Northern Pensions Research Group) (2002) *Response to Work and Pensions Committee inquiry into the future of UK pensions*, London: The Stationery Office.

Itzin, C. and Phillipson, C. (1993) *Age barriers at work: Maximising the potential of mature and older workers*, Solihull: Metropolitan Authorities Recruitment Agency.

Jacobs, S. (1999) 'Trends in women's career patterns and in gender occupational mobility in Britain', *Gender, Work and Organisation*, vol 6, no 1, pp 32-46.

Jepsen, M. and Meulders, D. (2002) 'The individualisation of rights in social protection systems', in H. Sarfati and G. Bonoli (eds) *Labour markets and social protection reforms in international perspective*, Aldershot: Ashgate.

Johnson, P. and Falkingham, J. (1992) *Ageing and economic welfare*, London: Sage Publications.

Jones, R. (2000) 'Mis-selling bill tops £13bn', *Guardian*, 2 December, Money Section.

Joshi, H. (1991) 'Sex and motherhood as handicaps in the labour market', in M. McLean and D. Groves (eds) *Women's issues in social policy*, London: Routledge, pp 179-93.

Joshi, H. (2000) 'Production, reproduction and education: women, children and work in contemporary Britain', Professorial Lecture at the Institute of Education, University of London, 29 June.

Joshi, H. and Davies, H. (1992) *Childcare and mothers' lifetime earnings: Some European contrasts*, London: Centre for Economic Policy Research.

Kay, W. (2002) 'Danger looms for the vulnerable low-paid saver', *Independent*, 10 August, www.independent.co.uk/story.jsp?story=322943.

Labour Party (1997) 'Tories have betrayed pensioners', Press release published in February, London: Labour Party.

LaValle, I., Finch, S., Nove, A. and Lewin, C. (2000) 'Parents' demand for childcare', *Labour Market Trends*, June, pp 293-5.

Leitner, S. (2001) 'Sex and gender discrimination within EU pension systems', *Journal of European Social Policy*, vol 11, no 2, pp 99-115.

Lister, R. (1994) '"She has other duties" – women, citizenship and social security', in S. Baldwin and J. Falkingham (eds) *Social security and social change: New challenges to the Beveridge model,* Hemel Hempstead: Harvester Wheatsheaf.

Liu, L. (1999) 'Retirement income security in the United Kingdom', *Social Security Bulletin*, vol 62, no 1, pp 23-46.

Mabbett, D. (1997) *Pension funding: Economic imperative or political strategy*, Discussion Paper 97/1, Uxbridge: Brunel University.

McDonald, P. (2000) 'The "toolbox" of public policies to impact on fertility – a global view', in C. Bagavos and C. Martin (eds) Synthesis Report on Annual Seminar held in Seville, 15-16 September, Vienna: Austrian Institute for Family Studies/European Observatory on Family Matters.

McKnight, A., Elias, P. and Wilson, R. (1998) *Low pay and the National Insurance system: A statistical picture*, Manchester: Equal Opportunities Commission.

McRae, S. (1993) 'Returning to work after childbirth: opportunities and inequalities', *European Sociological Review*, vol 9, no 2, pp 125-37.

McRae, S. (forthcoming) 'Constraints and choices in mothers' employment careers: a consideration of Hakim's preference theory', *Sociology*, submitted 2002.

Macran, S., Joshi, H. and Dex, S. (1996) 'Employment after childbearing: a survival analysis', *Work, Employment and Society*, vol 10, no 2, pp 273-96.

Mann, K. (2001) *Approaching retirement: Social divisions, welfare and exclusion*, Bristol: The Policy Press.

Mann, K. (2002) '"Faith in the city": absolving employers and protecting vested interests', in A. Deacon (ed) *Debating pensions. Self interest, citizenship and the common good*, London: Civitas, pp 79-93.

Marsh, A., Ford, R. and Finlayson, J. (1997) *Lone parents, work and benefits*, London: DSS/PSI.

Marsh, A., McKay, S., Smith, A. and Stephenson, A. (2001) *Low income families in Britain. Work, welfare and social security in 1999*, DSS Research Report no 138, London: DSS/CDS, and personal communication from A. Marsh based on special analysis of the 1999 data.

Mercer, W. (2002) 'End of the party', *Economist*, 2 March.

Millar, J. (2002) 'Adjusting welfare policies to stimulate job entry: the example of the United Kingdom', in H. Sarfati and G. Bonoli (eds) *Labour market and social protection reforms in international perspective*, Aldershot: Ashgate.

Minns, R. (2001) *The cold war in welfare: Stock markets versus pensions*, London: Verso.

Modood, T. and Berthoud, R. (eds) (1997) *Ethnic minorities in Britain. Diversity and disadvantage*, London: Policy Studies Institute.

Mullan, P. (2000) *The imaginary time bomb: Why an ageing population is not a social problem*, London: I.B. Tauris.

Murgatroyd, L. and Neuberger, H. (1997) A *household satellite account for the UK*, London: The Stationery Office.

Murthi, M., Orszag, M. and Orszag, P. (2001) 'Administrative costs under a decentralised approach to individual accounts: lessons from the United Kingdom', in R. Holzmann and J. Stiglitz (eds) *New ideas about old age security*, Washington, DC: World Bank/Oxford University Press.

NAO (National Audit Office) (1990) *The elderly: Information requirements for supporting the implications of personal pensions for the National Insurance Fund*, HC 55, London: HMSO.

NAPF (National Association of Pension Funds) (1996) *NAPF annual survey 1995*, London: NAPF.

NAPF (2002) *Pensions – Plain and simple*, London: NAPF.

NCOPF (National Council for One Parent Families) (2001) www.oneparentfamilies.org.uk.

Nesbitt, S. and Neary, D (2001) *Ethnic minorities and their pension decisions: A study of Pakistani, Bangladeshi and white men in Oldham*, York: Joseph Rowntree Foundation.

O'Connor, S., Orloff, A. and Shaver, S. (1999) *States, markets, families: Gender, liberalism and social policy in Australia, Canada, Great Britain and the United States*, Cambridge: Cambridge University Press.

OECD (Organisation for Economic Co-operation and Development) (2000) *Employment outlook*, Paris: OECD.

OECD (2001a) *OECD health data 2001*, CD-Rom, Paris: OECD.

OECD (2001b) *Employment outlook*, Paris: OECD.

ONS (Office for National Statistics) (1997) *Social Security Statistics 1997*, London: The Stationery Office.

ONS (1999) *Population Trends 98*, Winter, London: The Stationery Office.

ONS (2000a) *Living in Britain: Results from the General Household Survey 1998*, London: ONS.

ONS (2000b) *Marriage, Divorce and Adoption Statistics 1998*, London: The Stationery Office.

ONS (2001) *New Earnings Survey 1975 and 2000*, London: The Stationery Office.

ONS (2002a) *The UK 2000 Time Use Survey*, www.statistics.gov.uk/themes/ social_finances/TimeUseSurvey/.

ONS (2002b) *Social Trends 32*, London: The Stationery Office (also available at www.statistics.gov.uk/downloads/theme_social/Social_Trends32/ Social_Trends32.pdf).

ONS (2002c) *Living in Britain. Results from the 2001 General Household Survey*, London: The Stationery Office (also available at www.statistics.gov.uk/).

ONS (2002d) *Population Trends 110*, Winter, London: The Stationery Office.

O'Reilly, J. and Fagan, C. (eds) (1998) *Part-time prospects*, London: Routledge.

Owen, D. (1994) *Ethnic minority women and the labour market: Analysis of the 1991 Census*, EOC Research Series, Manchester: Equal Opportunities Commission.

Paci, P., Joshi, H. and Makepeace, G. (1995) 'Pay gaps facing men and women born in 1958: differences in the labour market', in J. Humphries and J. Rubery (eds) *The economics of equal opportunities*, Manchester: Equal Opportunities Commission.

Parker, H. (ed) (2000) *Low cost but acceptable incomes for older people. A minimum income standard for households aged 65-74 years in the UK*, Bristol: The Policy Press.

Pascall, G. and Lewis, J. (2000) 'Care work: can we better Beveridge?', *Social Policy Association News*, Feb/Mar, pp 16-17.

Peggs, K. (1995) *Women and pensions*, PhD thesis, Guildford: Sociology Department, University of Surrey.

Peggs, K. (2000) 'Which pension? Women, risk and pension choice', *The Sociological Review*, vol 48, no 3, pp 349-64.

Phillips, L. (1998) 'Hegemony and political discourse: the lasting impact of Thatcherism', *Sociology*, vol 32, no 4, pp 847-67.

Pickering, A. (2002) *A simpler way to better pensions: An independent report*, London: Department of Work and Pensions.

Pierson, P. (ed) (2001) *The new politics of the welfare state*, Oxford: Oxford University Press.

Plender, J. (2003) 'Please sir, must I have even less?', *Financial Times*, 18/19 January, Money Section, p 1.

PPG (Pensions Provision Group) (1998) *We all need pensions: The prospects for pension provision*, London: The Stationery Office.

PPI (Pensions Policy Institute) (2003) *The pensions landscape*, London: PPI.

PRA (Pre-Retirement Association) and HtA (Help the Aged) (1997) *Women and pensions*, London: Help the Aged.

Price, D. (2003) 'Pension sharing on divorce: the future for women', in C. Bochel, N. Ellison and M. Powell (eds) *Social Policy Review 15*, Bristol: The Policy Press.

Price, D. and Ginn, J. (2003) 'Sharing the crust? Gender, partnership status and inequalities in pension accumulation', in S. Arber, K. Davidson and J. Ginn (eds) *Gender and ageing: Changing roles and relationships*, Buckingham: Open University Press.

Rake, K. with Davies, H., Joshi, H. and Alami, R. (2000) *Women's incomes over the lifetime*, London: The Stationery Office.

Ring, P. (2002) 'The implications of the "New Insurance Contract" for UK pension provision: rights, responsibilities and risks', *Critical Social Policy*, vol 22, no 4, pp 551-71.

Rowlingson, K. (2002) 'Private pension planning: the rhetoric of responsibility, the reality of insecurity', *Journal of Social Policy*, vol 31, no 4, pp 623-42.

Sainsbury, S. (1996) *Gender, equality and welfare states*, Cambridge: Cambridge University Press.

St John, S. and Gran, B. (2001) 'The world's social laboratory: women-friendly aspects of New Zealand pensions', in J. Ginn, D. Street and S. Arber (eds) *Women, work and pensions: International issues and prospects*, Buckingham: Open University Press.

Sandler, R. (2002) *Medium and long-term retail savings in the UK*, London: Department of Work and Pensions.

Shaw, C. (1999) '1996-based population projections by legal marital status for England and Wales', *Population Trends*, and personal communication from John Haskey, Office for National Statistics, February 2002.

Shragge, E. (1984) *Pensions policy in Britain: A socialist analysis*, London: Routledge & Kegan Paul.

Sinfield, A. (1978) 'Analyses in the social division of welfare', *Journal of Social Policy*, vol 72, pp 129-56.

Sinfield, A. (2000) 'Tax benefits in non-state pensions', *European Journal of Social Security*, vol 2, no 2, pp 137-67.

Sinfield, A. (2002) 'The cost and unfairness of pension tax incentives', Memorandum PEN 61, House of Commons Work and Pensions Committee, *The future of UK pensions*, First Report of Session 2002-2003, volume III, HC 92-III, pp 300-5.

Sloane, P. (1990) 'Use of equal opportunities legislation and earnings differentials: a comparative study', *Industrial Relations Journal*, vol 21, no 3, pp 221-9.

Smart, B. (1999) *Facing modernity: Ambivalence, reflexivity and morality*, London: Sage Publications.

Social Security Committee (2000) *Pensioner poverty*, London: The Stationery Office.

Stafford, B. (1998) *National Insurance and the contributory principle*, DSS In-house report no 39, London: DSS.

Street, D. and Ginn, J. (2001) 'The demographic debate: the gendered political economy of pensions', in J. Ginn, D. Street and S. Arber (eds) *Women, work and pensions: International issues and prospects*, Buckingham: Open University Press.

Sutherland, H. (1998) *A citizen's pension*, Microsimulation Unit Discussion Paper MU9804, Department of Applied Economics, Cambridge: University of Cambridge.

Taskinen, S. (2000) 'Alternative child-care policies and fertility', in C. Bagavos and C. Martin (eds) *Low fertility, families and public policies*, Synthesis Report on Annual Seminar held in Seville, September 15-16, Vienna: Austrian Institute for Family Studies/European Observatory on Family Matters.

Thane, P. (1978) 'The muddled history of retiring at 60 and 65', *New Society*, 3 August, pp 234-6.

The Work Foundation (2003) 'Response to the Pensions Green Paper *Simplicity, security and choice*', www.theworkfoundation.com/.

Titmuss, R. (1958) *Essays on the welfare state*, London: Allen & Unwin.

Toynbee, P. (2003) *Hard work*, London: Bloomsbury.

Trades Union Congress (2002) *Prospects for pensions*, London: TUC.

Wachman, R. (2002) 'Riding out the big dipper', *Observer*, 21 July, Business Section, p 3.

Waine, B. (1995) 'A disaster foretold? The case of the personal pension', *Social Policy and Administration*, vol 29, no 4, pp 317-34.

Walby, S. (ed) (1999) *New agendas for women*, Basingstoke: Macmillan.

Walker, A. (1990) 'The economic "burden" of ageing and the prospect of intergenerational conflict', *Ageing and Society*, vol 10, pp 377-96.

Walker, A. and Maltby, T. (1997) *Ageing Europe*, Buckingham: Open University Press.

Walker, A., Alber, J. and Guillemard, A.-M. (1993) *Older people in the EU: Social and economic policies*, Brussels: CEC.

Walker, R., Heaver, C. and McKay, S. (2000) *Building up pension rights*, Research Report no 114, London: DSS.

Ward, P. (1996) *The great British pensions robbery*, Preston: Waterfall Books.

Ward, C., Dale, A. and Joshi, H. (1996) 'Combining employment with children: an escape from dependence?', *Journal of Social Policy*, vol 25, no 2, pp 223-48.

Warner, J. (2002) 'Outlook: a pensions mess that the government just keeps ducking', *Independent*, 23 November, www.independent.co.uk/story.jsp?story=354963.

Wilkinson, M. (1993) 'British tax policy 1979-90: equity and efficiency', *Policy & Politics*, vol 21, no 3, pp 207-17.

Willetts, D. (2002) 'Frank Field's superfund: misusing the power of the state', in A. Deacon (ed) *Debating pensions. Self interest, citizenship and the common good*, London: Civitas, pp 47-56.

Williams, T. and Field, J. (1993) *Pension choices: A survey of personal pensions in comparison with other pension options*, Department of Social Security Research Paper no 22, London: HMSO.

Work and Pensions Committee (2002) *The future of UK pensions. First report of session 2002-2003*, Vol III, HC92-III, London: The Stationery Office.

Wynn, S. (2001) http://www.stakeholder.cwc.net.

Statistical tables

Table A3.1: Employment status of men and women by ethnicity and age group (column percentages)

		White	Indian	Black	Chinese/ other	Pakistani	Bangla- deshi
Men 20-59							
N=		43,706	725	683	626	429	139
20s	FT employed	65.5	46.1	38.9	32.8	40.9	42.9
	Self-employed	8.0	6.7	4.1	2.7	7.3	4.8
	PT employed	3.5	4.2	9.3	5.9	5.1	7.1
	Not employed	23.1	43.0	47.7	58.6	46.7	45.2
	N=	102,90	165	193	186	137	42
30s	FT employed	70.1	64.9	48.8	43.0	36.7	38.8
	Self-employed	14.0	17.5	8.1	14.0	20.3	10.2
	PT employed	1.9	1.8	2.1	6.8	7.8	12.2
	Not employed	13.9	15.8	41.1	36.2	35.2	38.8
	N=	12,576	228	285	235	128	49
40s	FT employed	65.9	57.8	57.3	54.3	27.4	21.1
	Self-employed	16.6	20.4	7.7	18.6	19.8	21.1
	PT employed	2.0	1.9	6.0	3.1	4.7	10.5
	Not employed	15.5	19.9	29.1	24.0	48.1	47.4
	N=	11,461	211	117	129	106	19
50s	FT employed	51.9	43.8	53.4	48.0	20.7	10.3
	Self-employed	16.0	19.8	3.4	14.7	19.0	3.4
	PT employed	2.9	1.7	1.1	4.0	1.7	17.2
	Not employed	29.1	34.7	42.0	33.3	58.6	69.0
	N=	9,377	121	88	75	58	29

Table A3.1: Employment status of men and women by ethnicity and age group (column percentages) (continued)

		White	Indian	Black	China/other	Pakistani	Bangla-deshi
Women 20-59							
N=		47,054	809	947	734	466	171
20s	FT employed	45.7	33.8	32.7	25.3	12.2	3.9
	Self-employed	2.4	3.7	0.7	1.3	3.3	0
	PT employed	16.2	14.4	10.7	9.6	10.5	6.5
	Not employed	35.7	48.1	56.0	63.8	74.0	89.6
	N=	11,654	216	300	229	181	77
30s	FT employed	31.7	35.9	39.2	23.9	6.1	2.3
	Self-employed	5.0	8.5	2.4	8.3	2.0	4.5
	PT employed	29.6	19.2	14.1	16.5	9.5	2.3
	Not employed	33.7	36.3	44.3	51.3	82.4	90.9
	N=	13,711	281	375	230	148	44
40s	FT employed	36.0	36.3	43.7	37.1	5.6	3.2
	Self-employed	6.4	7.4	2.6	6.7	3.4	3.2
	PT employed	31.4	19.5	14.6	16.9	10.1	6.5
	Not employed	26.2	36.7	39.1	39.3	80.9	87.1
	N=	11,810	215	151	178	89	31
50s	FT employed	25.3	18.6	35.5	23.7	4.2	0
	Self-employed	4.9	8.2	3.3	5.2	0	0
	PT employed	27.2	8.2	15.7	15.5	2.1	5.3
	Not employed	42.6	64.9	45.5	55.7	93.8	94.7
	N=	9,879	97	121	97	48	19

Note: Percentages in italics indicate base < 30.

Source: Ginn and Arber (2001), using data from Family Resources Surveys 1994-96

Table A3.2: Odds ratios for contributing to a private pension by ethnicity, men aged 20-59

	Base model	Model 2	Model 3	Model 4	Model 5
Ethnicity	+++	+++	+++	+++	+++
White	1.00	1.00	1.00	1.00	1.00
Black	0.32**	0.38**	0.32**	0.50**	0.59**
Indian	0.51**	0.30**	0.35**	0.37**	0.47**
Chinese/other	0.30**	0.45**	0.23**	0.34**	0.40**
Pakistani	0.12**	0.11**	0.10**	0.15**	0.21**
Bangladeshi	0.06**	0.05**	0.05**	0.07**	0.11**
Marital status		+++	+++	+++	+++
Married		1.00	1.00	1.00	1.00
Single		0.39**	0.37**	0.68**	0.80**
Widowed		0.46**	0.48**	0.80	0.81
Divorced/separated		0.35**	0.36**	0.65**	0.69**
Parental status		+++	+++	++	++
Youngest child 0-9		1.00	1.00	1.00	1.00
Youngest child 10+		1.36**	1.37**	1.16**	1.15**
No dependent child		1.24**	1.27**	1.10*	1.15**
Age finished full-time education			+++	+++	+++
Under 16 yrs			1.00	1.00	1.00
16 yrs			1.64**	1.37**	1.17**
17-18 yrs			2.53**	2.11**	1.44**
Over 19 yrs			2.70**	3.42**	1.74**
Employment status				+++	+++
Full-time employee				1.00	1.00
Part-time employee				0.18**	0.29**
Self-employed				0.40**	0.61**
Not employed				0.00**	0.00**
Years employed full-time				+++	+++
Less than 5				1.00	1.00
5-9				3.35**	2.83**
10-19				5.82**	4.53**
20+				10.45**	7.33**

Table A3.2: Odds ratios for contributing to a private pension by ethnicity, men aged 20-59 (continued)

	Base model	Model 2	Model 3	Model 4	Model 5
Socioeconomic group					+++
Professionals/large managers					1.00
Intermediate non-manual/small managers					0.73**
Routine non-manual					0.87*
Employers/self-employed					0.60**
Skilled manual					0.62**
Semi-skilled manual					0.53**
Unskilled manual					0.59**
Not employed/Armed Forces/not known					1.04
Gross income, £/wk					+++
Less than 50					1.00
50-99					0.95
100-199					1.07
200-299					2.00**
300+					3.97**
G sq (Null)	62,073				
Change in G sq	4,201	1,133	1,503	19,961	1,755
Change in df	12	3	5	6	11
N = 46,044					

Notes: * Significance of difference from reference category; * $p < 0.05$, ** $p < 0.01$.

+ Significance of variable in improving the model; + $p < 0.05$, ++ $p < 0.01$, +++ $p < 0.001$.

All models include a variable for five-year age group, not shown.

Source: Ginn and Arber (2001), using data from Family Resources Surveys 1994-96

Table A3.3: Odds ratios for contributing to a private pension by ethnicity, women aged 20-59

	Base model	Model 2	Model 3	Model 4	Final model
Ethnicity	+++	+++	+++	+++	+++
White	1.00	1.00	1.00	1.00	1.00
Black	0.74**	0.85*	0.72**	0.75**	0.73**
Indian	0.59**	0.59**	0.47**	0.50**	0.59**
Chinese/other	0.51**	0.54**	0.41**	0.54**	0.57**
Pakistani	0.12**	0.13**	0.14**	0.61	0.64
Bangladeshi	0.07**	0.07**	0.07**	0.37	0.43
Marital status		+++	+++	+++	+++
Married		1.00	1.00	1.00	1.00
Single		0.68**	0.63**	0.74**	0.67**
Widowed		0.73**	0.78**	0.98	0.61**
Divorced/separated		0.65**	0.70**	0.83**	0.62**
Parental status		+++	+++	+++	+++
Youngest child 0-9		1.00	1.00	1.00	1.00
Youngest child 10+		2.15**	2.19**	1.19**	1.12*
No dependent child		3.90**	4.07**	1.44**	1.50**
Age ended full-time education			+++	+++	+++
Under 16 yrs			1.00	1.00	1.00
16 yrs			1.70**	1.45**	1.16**
17-18 yrs			3.18**	2.44**	1.55**
Over 19 yrs			3.92**	4.18**	1.82**
Employment status				+++	+++
Full-time employee				1.00	1.00
Part-time employee				0.32**	0.68**
Self-employed				0.22**	0.48**
Not employed				0.00**	0.00**
Years employed full-time				+++	+++
Less than 5				1.00	1.00
5-9				1.99**	1.76**
10-19				3.10**	2.39**
20+				4.84**	3.22**

Table A3.3: Odds ratios for contributing to a private pension by ethnicity, women aged 20-59 (continued)

	Base model	Model 2	Model 3	Model 4	Final model
Socioeconomic group					+++
Professionals/large managers					1.00
Intermediate non-manual/small managers					0.92
Routine non-manual					0.82**
Employers/self-employed					0.84**
Skilled manual					0.64**
Semi-skilled manual					0.51**
Unskilled manual					0.63**
Not employed/Armed forces/not known					0.97
Gross income, £/wk					+++
Less than 50					1.00
50-99					1.50**
100-199					3.43**
200-299					7.05**
300+					13.05**
G sq (Null)	65,093				
Change in G sq	1,500	2,820	2,301	21,135	2,578
Change in df	12	5	3	6	11
N = 49,917					

Notes: * Significance of difference from reference category; * p<0.05, ** p<0.01.
+ Significance of variable in improving the model; + p<0.05, ++ p<0.01, +++ p<0.001.
All models include a variable for 5-year age group, not shown.

Source: Ginn and Arber (2001), using data from Family Resources Surveys 1994-96

Table A5.1: Percentage of employees contributing to a private pension by educational level and hours of work of women, men and women aged 20-59

	Men	Women		
Educational level		**All**	**FT**[a]	**PT**
Degree/equivalent and above	87	74	83	55
A level/equivalent	77	56	65	39
O level/GCSE	77	55	71	37
Other qualifications	73	47	61	32
No qualifications	71	37	57	24
N	10,213	10,961	6,038	4,922

Note: [a] Full-time employment is defined as 31+ hours per week usually worked.

Source: Ginn and Arber (2002), using data from GHS 1994-96

Table A5.2: (a) Percentage employed and (b) percentage employed full time[a] by lifecourse category and educational level, women aged 20-59

Lifecourse category	(a) % employed					(b) % employed full time				
	Degree +	A levels	O/ GCSE	Other	None	Degree +	A levels	O/ GCSE	Other	None
All women	81	76	72	65	53	55	50	39	33	22
Never had child <35	92	91	90	81	63	84	82	79	69	52
Child 0-4	70	54	51	42	26	29	21	15	12	6
Child 5-9	81	72	69	58	43	40	21	19	21	10
Child 10-15	87	84	78	77	63	47	33	30	29	20
Child 16+	75	76	76	74	58	46	47	40	37	25
Never had child 35+	81	81	83	67	57	69	71	63	51	37
Cramer's V	*0.21*	*0.33*	*0.31*	*0.30*	*0.24*	*0.41*	*0.54*	*0.49*	*0.37*	*0.24*
Under age 35										
Never had child	92	91	90	81	63	84	82	79	69	52
Child 0-4	69	53	50	40	25	31	21	15	10	5
Phi	*0.30*	*0.44*	*0.44*	*0.40*	*0.34*	*0.52*	*0.60*	*0.65*	*0.62*	*0.53*

Notes: $p < .001$ at each educational level. [a] Full-time employment is defined as 31+ hours per week usually worked. Full-time students excluded from the analysis. For base numbers see Table A5.5.

Source: Ginn and Arber (2002), using data from GHS 1994-96

Table A5.3: Median gross earnings (£ per week), by lifecourse category and educational level, all women aged 20-59, including those not employed[a]

Lifecourse category	Degree+	A levels	O/GCSE	Other	None	All
All women	220	131	85	60	14	77
Never had child <35	272	191	179	156	92	196
Child 0-4	120	15	0	0	0	0
Child 5-9	150	75	49	29	0	42
Child 10-15	231	115	88	71	40	80
Child 16+	191	134	100	91	35	69
Never had child 35+	300	215	192	129	53	162

Note: [a] Full-time students excluded from the analysis.

Source: Ginn and Arber (2002), using data from GHS 1994-96

Table A5.4: Percentage contributing to a private pension, by lifecourse category and educational level, all women aged 20-59[a]

Lifecourse category	Degree+	A levels	O/GCSE	Other	None
All women	61	48	41	34	22
Never had child <35	65	54	58	39	26
Child 0-4	55	38	28	22	7
Child 5-9	54	38	26	23	10
Child 10-15	62	46	41	35	19
Child 16+	60	48	45	40	27
Never had child 35+	72	70	63	51	35
Cramer's V	*0.11*	*0.18*	*0.27*	*0.20*	*0.21*
Under age 35					
Never had child	65	54	58	39	26
Child 0-4	54	37	27	19	6
Phi	*0.11*	*0.16*	*0.32*	*0.22*	*0.28*

Notes: p<.001 at each educational level. [a] Full-time students excluded from the analysis.

Source: Ginn and Arber (2002), using data from GHS 1994-96

Table A5.5: Base numbers of women aged 20-59[a] by lifecourse category and educational qualifications

Lifecourse category	Degree+	A levels	O/GCSE	Other	None	All	% in each lifestage
Never had child <35	831	586	921	294	171	2,803	16
Youngest child 0-4	624	403	1,204	547	687	3,465	20
Youngest child 5-9	375	224	659	354	557	2,169	13
Youngest child 10-15	363	154	565	324	742	2,148	13
No child under 16	650	253	1,011	733	2,479	5,126	30
Never had child, 35+	371	117	339	196	399	1,422	8
All aged 20-59	3,214	1,737	4,699	2,448	5,035	17,133	
% in each qualifications group	19	10	27	14	29	100	
All aged <35	1,303	1,021	2,321	954	988	6,587	
% in each qualifications group	20	16	35	14	15	100	

Note: [a] Full-time students excluded.

Source: Ginn and Arber (2002), using data from GHS 1994-96

Table A6.1: Percentage employed[a] full and part time[b] in eight EU countries (1990, 1995, 2000)

	Women						Men					
	Full-time			Part-time			Full-time			Part-time		
	1990	1995	2000	1990	1995	2000	1990	1995	2000	1990	1995	2002
Sweden	61	54	57	20	17	15	81	69	71	5	5	6
Denmark	50	50	55	21	17	17	72	73	74	8	8	7
France	39	39	41	11	13	13	67	63	65	3	4	4
Britain	38	37	39	25	25	27	78	71	73	4	6	7
Germany	37	39	38	16	16	20	74	71	71	2	3	4
Ireland	29	30	36	8	11	17	65	62	70	3	4	6
Italy	30	28	30	7	8	9	69	63	64	3	3	4
Netherlands	22	24	27	25	29	36	65	66	71	10	9	11

Notes: [a] as % of population aged 15-64 (16-64 in Britain and Sweden). [b] usually worked less than 30 hours/week.

Break in series after 1990 for Sweden, Denmark, Germany and Italy.

Source: Calculated from OECD (2000; 2001) Tables A and E

Table A6.2 Comparing incomes of older people across countries (EU15)

a) Poverty rate (% of those aged 65+ with less than 60% of national median income)

b) Median income of those aged 65+ as % of median income of those aged 0-64

	EU15	NL	L	S	D	I	E	FIN	F	UK	B	A	DK	P	EL	IRE
a)	17	7	8	8	11	14	16	17	19	21	22	24	31	33	33	34
b)	89	93	99	83	97	96	91	78	90	78	76	84	68	76	74	69

Source: CEC 2003, Table 2, based on European Community Household Panel Survey data for 1998, income equivalised to adjust for household size

Index